Amusement Park 9-1-1

Stories of Death, Debauchery & Disaster From An Amusement Park Near You

By Kermit Gonzalo

Copyright © 2014 Kermit Gonzalo

ISBN-13: 9781502362148

ISBN-10: 1502362147

All rights reserved.

No part of this book may be used or reproduced in any matter whatsoever without written permission except in the case of brief quotations embodied in critical articles and journals.

This book makes reference to various copyrights and trademarks of the Universal Studios Theme Parks, Six Flags Entertainment Corporation, SeaWorld Parks and Entertainment, Cedar Fair Entertainment Company; this book is in no way authorized by, endorsed by or affiliated with these companies or their subsidiaries.
The mention of names and places associated with these companies and their businesses are not intended in any way to infringe on any existing or registered trademarks but are used in context for educational purposes.

The author and publisher are not affiliated with nor a representative of the specific companies, organizations, or authorities in this book. The opinions and statements expressed in this book are solely those of the author and/or people quoted by the author and do not reflect the opinions and policies of the specific companies mentioned.

While every precaution has been taken in the preparation of this book, neither the author nor publisher assumes responsibility for errors or omissions. Neither is any liability assumed for damages resulting, or alleged to result, directly or indirectly from the use of the information contained herein.

First Printing, 2014
Questions or Comments: kermitgonzalo@gmail.com

CONTENTS

Introduction 1
Universal Studios 5
SeaWorld 25
Six Flags 41
Busch Gardens 89
Regional Favorites 99
Bibliography 115
About the Author 133

INTRODUCTION:

Each year in the United States roughly 300 million people visit an amusement park. These folks enjoy nearly 2 billion rides on attractions that range from tame to terror filled. According to the National Safety Council, and the International Association of Amusement Parks and Attractions, of these 2 billion annual rides there were roughly 1,500 ride-related injuries.

The stories shared in this book are some of those accidents. Obviously, not every accident will be discussed, only the more notable ones. The ones that made headlines or resulted in some sort of safety change due to the accident will be included here. This book will also glance at some of the other unsavory situations that happen in an amusement park setting—murder, death, sex offenses, animal attacks, theft and other scandalous tales.

All of this leads to a very basic question. Who doesn't enjoy visiting an amusement park? The statistics above tell us an overwhelming amount of people do. Amusement parks are almost as American as apple pie, something America didn't invent, but whole-heartedly embraces. The same can be said for amusement parks. We didn't create them but certainly celebrate and fine-tuned them to our liking.

The earliest resemblance of an amusement park dates back to Dyrehavsbakken, near Copenhagen, Denmark in 1583. Two and a half centuries later in 1843 came Tivoli Gardens, also in Denmark. Each of these parks is still operating today and are examples of what our country calls a fixed-site amusement park.

Kermit Gonzalo

American history is filled with fixed-site parks. From Steeplechase Park at Coney Island, opening before the turn of the twentieth century to the extravagant and technology filled thrill producers such as Disney, Universal Studios and Six Flags. If the amusement park and their attractions are permanent and not on the move like a carnival or county fair, then as the name suggests, the park is considered a fixed site.

Today, America has some four hundred of these parks nationwide. More than likely you've visited one or have one within driving distance to your home. They truly are everywhere, and accidents don't discriminate according to location. For our discussion, the amusement park accident statistics mentioned are exclusively for fixed-site parks. Contrary to popular belief, there really are no wide-ranging government laws on the federal level regulating these parks.

With the Consumer Product Safety Act signed into law by President Nixon in 1972, the government oversees non-permanent amusement parks, such as carnivals and fairs. However, under this act the federal government has no authority to regulate or inspect fixed-site parks. People in the industry and government refer to this as the "Roller Coaster Loophole."

This loophole is something the large fixed-site park owners would like to keep in place. All of the big names in the industry lobby to keep their freedom, and so far have been successful. This success has been due in part to some pre-emptive voluntary measures they've adopted.

Voluntary measures aside, it doesn't mean legislators haven't tried to regulate the industry over the years. As recently as 2007 and 2011, Massachusetts Senator Edward Markey tried in vain to get the National Amusement Park Ride Safety Act passed. The act would have allowed the federal government to inspect and oversee fixed sight venues in conjunction with the roughly thirty states in the country that have laws regulating parks at the state level. Barring state level inspection, most parks are self-governing or rely on their insurance companies to inspect and ensure the safety of their rides. State level inspection or third party inspection doesn't necessarily mean things are always copasetic in the world of amusement park safety; accidents do happen.

As the industry statistics outline, the chance of being seriously injured on a ride at a fixed-site park in the U.S. is 1 in 24 million. The chance of being fatally injured is 1 in 750 million. As The International Association of Amusement Parks and Attractions will highlight, this is one of the safer forms of recreational activities in the country.

Based upon these statistics, amusement parks are very safe. According to the National Safety Council in 2014, you are much more likely to die on your way to the amusement park (odds are 1 in 112 for a fatal car crash) than while at one. As you will come to find out, many of these accidents usually fall into one of three categories: rider error, operator error or death / injury as a result of a pre-existing health condition (usually involving the heart or brain and unknown to the person prior to the ride).

With the latter in mind, a portion of the proceeds from each copy of Amusement Park 9-1-1 is donated to the American Heart and American Stroke Foundation. All right, the background is set. We are going to look at some of the bigger names in the amusement park industry: Universal Studios, Sea World, Six Flags, Busch Gardens and some other regional favorites. Disney, however, is excluded from the book. As the leader in amusement park visits with nearly 130 million annually, Disney certainly has their fair share of accidents and incidents. These stories are worthy of their own volume and will be published in the near future.

Before we begin, sympathies and condolences to the families who set out for a day of fantasy and fun, and ended up submerged in a nightmare. Without further ado, we are off to see Harry Potter and hear about the events at Universal Studios.

UNIVERSAL STUDIOS

The Universal Studios amusement parks in Hollywood, California and Orlando, Florida, both have their origins with the world famous movie studio in California. As early as 1915, folks could pay a small fee and gain admission to Universal Studio's back lot and witness the inner workings of a real movie studio.

This glimpse into show business continues today with Universal Studio's back stage tour in Hollywood. In addition to the tour, there is an amusement park and Universal's CityWalk, a three-block area with shopping, entertainment and dining. Each one of these venues offers the public a unique and popular form of entertainment, entertainment that from time to time escalated into situations Universal probably wished was only featured in one of their movies, and not a real life experience for their customers or employees.

As mentioned, the studio back lot or tram tour was Universal's first foray into welcoming the public into their studio. Usually, the tours ran exclusively during the day. However, in 1986 that changed due to Halloween. That season the studio tour in the evening was dubbed "Halloween Horror Night." Passengers on the tram tour would see the same movie sets as the tours during the day, but once the evening rolled around, the scenes were decked out for the holiday complete with monsters, zombies and some trickery.

As one of the tours started, twenty-year-old Paul, a studio employee, assumed his position at a horror scene in the midst of a number of fake corpses. As the tour passed Paul, he was told to lunge out of the scene and scare the passersby. When

Paul sprang into action, something went terribly wrong. He stumbled and was run over by the tram. He got caught between the third and fourth tramcars and was dragged 100 feet. The young man was pronounced dead at the scene. The incident with Paul was deemed an accident and was the first death of its kind in the history of the tram tour.

Four years later, in November of 1990, another worker at Universal Studios in California found himself in an unfortunate situation. This time the situation was no accident. Michael, a security guard working at the studio, set fire to a paint shed. The fire quickly spread and destroyed four acres of sets (roughly 20 percent of the studio's outdoor sets) and part of the back lot tour.

The damage was estimated at $25 million, and Michael initially denied causing the fire. After hours of questioning, he finally admitted to it. Michael said he used a cigarette and a lighter to spark the fire in the shed where workers painted sets. Michael claimed he had a split personality and it was the other person inside of him that started the fire. His family contributed to the investigation and mentioned he was mentally disabled after being exposed to Agent Orange during the Vietnam War. In January of 1992, shortly before his trial was to start, Michael pled guilty and was sentenced to four years in prison.

The last story exclusive to the studio tram tour is also the most salacious. In December of 1992, thirty-year-old Wendy-Sue, a thirteen-year veteran employee at the tour, filed a $10 million sexual harassment lawsuit against the studio.

Wendy-Sue claimed management sexually harassed female employees for over a decade. She claimed managers repeatedly grabbed and pinched her breasts and buttocks. They displayed pornographic photos in work areas and routinely sought sexual favors from her.

Wendy-Sue claimed her two bosses trapped her in an office

where one of them masturbated in front of her. One manager even went as far as rubbing his erect penis against her body. If those acts weren't despicable enough, she was even offered a free vacation; all she had to do was sleep with the boss. Wendy-Sue wasn't the only victim. Nearly a dozen other women complained when the department was investigated. By September of 1993, Universal reached an out of court settlement with Wendy-Sue. Sources said she was paid $600,000, and per the agreement the company admitted no wrongdoing.

The studio tour itself wasn't the only property in Universal's portfolio to make headlines for the wrong reasons. Over at CityWalk, the company's entertainment complex was also the scene for some unsavory situations, and regretfully a handful of murders as well.

On Mother's Day in 1995, Paul took his two-year-old son, his mother, Doris, and the mother of his child, Sonia, to dinner at CityWalk. The family finished dinner and went back to their car on the fifth floor of the parking garage (a parking garage with no security cameras). Around the time Paul and his family left dinner, a call came into police and security. There was criminal activity happening on the upper floors of the garage.

Police and security entered the garage and walked the stairwell towards the top. At the fourth floor they found Paul lying on the ground covered in blood and moaning. He was mumbling something about his kid being upstairs and "they killed him." Police proceeded to the fifth floor where they saw blood everywhere and heard a child crying. The cries were from Paul's son, who was still strapped into his car seat and was calling out for his mother. Thankfully, the little guy was physically unharmed. The same couldn't be said for his mother, as she was one of the two lifeless bodies lying next to the car.

As the police surveyed the situation, Paul entered the fifth floor and identified the bodies. One was his mother and the other was the mother of his child. He then proceeded to pace and rock himself nervously. Police asked him if he was cut or stabbed anywhere. He told them no, but didn't know why he was covered in blood. Paul claimed at one point he was struck so hard he was knocked unconscious.

Officers started to question him about what exactly took place. He claimed the family was returning from dinner when someone shoved him from behind and demanded his money. Paul informed the robbers that he had no money. They stole his fanny pack anyway and pushed him to the ground. Once he stood up he saw his mother and Sonia lying on the ground covered in blood.

Paul didn't see what the attackers looked like and didn't know in which direction they fled. He did hear their voices and they were definitely male. Next, Paul said he ran down the stairs to get help, which is where police found him lying, covered in blood. Police documented Paul's story and the investigation was underway.

Five miles away and fifteen minutes later, another situation was unfolding for police. A distress call came in from a roadside highway call box. A woman named Donna initiated the call. Donna claimed she was robbed and stabbed there. When officers arrived, Donna was lying outside of her car, moaning. She was stabbed in the stomach so badly her intestines were exposed.

Donna's car doors were locked and the keys were inside the vehicle. An ambulance took her to the hospital and police investigated the scene. The investigation took police down the embankment past Donna's car where they found blood-covered handbags and a fanny pack. In addition there were blood-soaked rubber gloves and a knife--I'm sure you can see where this story is going.

Paul and Donna were boyfriend and girlfriend. The two planned the crime. They wanted to make it seem like a random robbery gone wrong. After police started to connect the dots, both Paul and Donna were arrested for murder. Obviously, both denied any involvement in the tragedy.

Police noted the evidence against each of them was insurmountable. There were parking garage ticket stubs with time stamps corroborating times, witnesses placing Donna at the scene and the victims' blood was everywhere. Paul and Donna pleaded not guilty to their charges, but a jury of their peers thought otherwise. In March of 1998, they were both found guilty. Paul was sentenced to death and Donna to life in prison. So, what was the motivation for this horrendous crime? Well, Paul thought his mother and Sonia were trying to keep him from seeing his son. In addition, his mother didn't approve of his relationship with Donna. Not to mention that Paul was allegedly having financial troubles and it was becoming difficult for him to meet his court ordered child support.

This crazy and horrendous incident aside, CityWalk is considered a very safe destination. Even the Los Angeles Police Department (LAPD) will tell you this. LAPD Commander, Andy Smith was quoted in 2014 as saying:

"I consider it a very safe place. I take my family there when they come to town. I've been to Universal CityWalk dozens of times off duty and have never had any issues."

The Commander's quote about CityWalk came from an article in the Los Angeles Times about a shootout there. In May of 2014, LAPD responded to a disturbance call around 1:00 P.M. at the Infusion Lounge. The club was having a DJ battle/contest that night. Tensions ran high, a fight ensued and bottles started to fly. Unfortunately, so did bullets.

When police arrived on scene they heard gunshots. Someone was firing indiscriminately into the crowd. Officers saw a suspect with a gun and fired upon him. It was twenty-one-year-old James. He was declared dead on the scene. As Commander

Smith said, Universal is safe, be it the tour, CityWalk or even their amusement park. As with each amusement park around the country, accidents happen, and Universal's park is no exception.

The park's incidents over the years have ranged from slip and falls, twisted ankles to dizziness and nausea. For the most part Universal Studios in Hollywood hasn't experienced an overwhelming number of fatal ride accidents. There were a few noteworthy incidents aboard one attraction, the Jurassic Park ride. In 1996, when the $110 million ride debuted, one hundred guests were sprayed with hydraulic fluid during a malfunction.

Four people were taken to the hospital with minor injuries. That same month, Marcy was aboard the ride, and she was spared the hydraulic fluid but suffered something worse. Marcy said she was injured from the jerking and rocking of the vehicle near the end of the ride. She said this movement injured her neck and required surgery. Marcy went on to sue Universal for her pain and damages. After a week-long trial, the jury sided with Marcy and found Universal at fault. They awarded her $90,000 ($50,000 for her medical bills and $40,000 for pain and suffering).

As it pertains to Universal Studios and their notable amusement park accidents, incidents and crimes, it seems as though more of the occurrences take place across the country in Florida. So why is this? Who knows? But let's speculate a bit— please, turn on your sarcasm detector for a moment.

The two Universal Parks, Hollywood and Orlando, have very similar yearly attendance rates. As of 2013 Hollywood had an attendance rate of 6.1 million visitors and Orlando had 7 million visitors. However, Universal Orlando does have the Islands of Adventure park that sees over 8 million people annually. So Orlando does see double the amount of people than its sister park in Hollywood.

Amusement Park 9-1-1

Islands of Adventure has numerous state-of-the-art thrill rides, which in turn could cause more accidents. Could this be the reason? Not necessarily; as the book will show, accidents can happen anywhere and anytime. Perhaps their problem is that cross-town rival, Mickey. Maybe he put one of his sorcerer apprentice curses on the park, á la Fantasia, for setting up shop near Disney's location.

Nah, come on, Harry Potter could squash that in a blink of an eye—but wait, maybe it *is* about location. Isn't there an old adage: location, location, location?

Perhaps some of the unfortunate things that take place from time to time at Universal Orlando really do have to do with their location in central Florida. You do know the park is located in an "urban high crime area" or at least that's what Universal claims.

This distinction is one that Universal embraces and therefore makes the company a recipient of $8 million in perfectly legal tax breaks. Who knew when the park opened in 1990 and Universal poured countless millions into their park, it would end up being considered a high crime area—you better watch your back when you're there!

In all seriousness, back in 1997, Florida legislators created the Urban High Crime Area Job Tax Credit. The credit allowed for counties in the state to nominate an area that has poverty, crime and unemployment at an extreme level. Businesses in these zones can apply for tax credits when they hire new employees. In 1998, Orlando's Mayor nominated parts of the city for inclusion into the credit. The area the Mayor included had some pretty rough stretches of town. In all, some 20 square miles were nominated and included into the Urban High Crime Area Job Tax Credit.

Years later, some of the areas included aren't so bad. Actually, some of them are down right prosperous, like the tracts Universal owns. Back in 2000 and 2001 Universal claimed $3.8 million in credits for the creation of their Islands of Adventure park, another $2 million in 2002 when they expanded their hotel enterprise and again in 2010 for $2.3 million with the expansion of Harry Potter. Universal's actions are not exactly what the state had in mind when they created the act, but it is perfectly legal.

Then again, judging by the next few stories, that whole "urban high crime area" could certainly be rationalized if need be—albeit more than likely with little success.

Late one evening in April of 2012, three employees were finishing up their shift at CityWalk Orlando's movie theatre. As they walked to their cars they noticed a woman passed out on top of an air conditioner and a man quickly buckling up his pants and scurrying away. The trio alerted a security guard who went over and investigated. The woman was face down; her skirt was around her waist and her underwear on the ground. The security officer promptly notified police and an ambulance.

The woman was transported to the hospital where she informed police she didn't recall how she got on the air conditioning unit. She said she did recall meeting a young man named Joshua who introduced himself as a professional golfer. When police tracked down Joshua and interviewed him, he told officers he met the young lady and three of her friends at the bar that evening. They danced and drank all night. Joshua even claimed he kissed the woman and performed a sex act on her while they danced together on the dance floor, all at her request. He told detectives both he and the accuser were drunk when they went outside to have consensual sex. The woman refuted the story and informed police she is a lesbian and would not willingly have sex with a man.

Another story of an unwanted sexual situation happened at Universal Orlando in May of 1999. This time it occurred between two employees. Thirty-one-year-old Juan, a restaurant employee, was arrested on three counts of sexual battery and one count of false imprisonment after he befriended a seventeen-year-old girl on a tram car at the park. The teen told police she was raped at an "employee's only" location in the park.

The stories don't get much better as we work our way through the Universal Studios deviant file. In April of 2002, Tanner was working as a greeter at the parks Spiderman ride when a family from New York approached him and asked him for assistance. Their four-year-old daughter needed to use the restroom and asked Tanner for directions. Tanner informed the family he would be happy to help them. He then proceeded to take the little girl into the men's employee bathroom where he touched her inappropriately. The girl came out and was visibly upset. She informed her parents what happened and police were called. Tanner was charged with sexual battery of a child and lewd and lascivious molestation of a child under the age of twelve. In an effort to keep the young girl from the stresses of a trial, a plea agreement was made. Tanner apologized and said he too was molested as a child. Tanner was sentenced to ten years in prison.

Universal was the scene for another sexually charged attack back in January of 2007. A thirty-two-year-old woman told police she was standing near the queue for the Revenge of the Mummy ride when she asked a man a question about the park. The man informed her that he could answer her question and asked that she follow him.

Once she started to follow the man, he grabbed her and dragged her into an emergency exit hallway. He threw her down and proceeded to bang her head against the ground. Once on the ground, he pinned her and started to take his pants off. He told her if she continued to scream, he would kill her.

Thankfully, she didn't listen to him. She continued to scream and fight back. She was eventually able to get free with only an abrasion on her head. Unfortunately, the attacker escaped. Universal complied with police to help apprehend the suspect. They even turned over any relevant surveillance, but it wasn't enough to apprehend the man.

The United States of America has many informal names and slogans. There is the famous land of the free, home of the brave. There is even the less patriotic land of second chances.

Well, a man once employed at Universal Orlando as none other than Captain America probably hopes the second slogan is true. Twenty-nine-year-old James donned his Captain America costume daily and mingled with park visitors. One day his mingling went a bit too far and got him arrested. In May of 2014, James was arrested and accused of allegedly sending sexual text messages along with pictures of his "little captain" to a sixteen-year-old girl.

When the girl's father learned of these messages he informed police. It seems James met the teenager while he was working in costume at the park. They took a picture together, she posted it online and James eventually saw it. He commented on the picture and the two began to chat as friends. Eventually, the conversation turned sexual. James allegedly sent 8 to 10 explicit photos to the girl, even after she commented that she was only sixteen years old. Things went a step further when the Captain and the minor made plans to meet up at a local mall. Before the two could have a date, police moved in and arrested the "super hero." This case is still pending.

Over the years the incidents at Universal certainly have run the gamut, and aren't exclusive to sexual deviance or murder. There has been a fair amount of other violence, disorderly conduct and bizarre behavior.

In April of 2011, thirty-three-year-old Adam was visiting CityWalk for his birthday. Shortly after midnight police claimed he started to pace and grab his head and face in front of the movie theatre he recently exited. They thought he was acting erratic and disorderly and went over to confront him. Police claimed the confrontation wasn't about arresting him, but perhaps to take him in for a mental health evaluation. When police approached Adam, they claimed the conversation escalated and became violent when he resisted them. As Adam allegedly put up a struggle with police, one of the officers started tasering him with a stun gun.

Shortly after, Adam became unresponsive. Police began to administer CPR but to no avail. Adam was pronounced dead at the hospital. Months later, the autopsy and toxicology report stated there were no alcohol or drugs in Adam's system. The medical examiner ruled his cause of death a homicide. Adam suffered sudden cardiac arrest from the tasering. He was shocked multiple times and for many seconds; 31 seconds, 5 seconds, 4 seconds and 5 seconds. Adam's family has since filed a wrongful death suit against the police department. The case is still ongoing.

Roughly a month after Adam's unfortunate night, the police and security teams at Universal had their hands full again with another birthday guest. Nancy was celebrating her fortieth birthday at Universal Studios in May of 2011. As Nancy's birthday evening progressed, she allegedly became drunk and got into an argument with her husband.

Police on site asked her to quiet down and leave the park. After being asked several times to leave, police and security claimed she became verbally abusive towards them (allegedly launching a slew of gay slurs and profanity at them). The officers escorted Nancy and her husband to their car in the parking garage in an effort to send them on their way.

The verbal abuse apparently didn't stop as the police were writing up a trespass warning for the couple at their car. At this point, things took a turn for the worse and police decided to lock Nancy up. The officers claimed that when they went to apprehend and handcuff Nancy, she resisted arrest and twisted around. This prompted them to use force, which led to Nancy breaking her arm (days after her arrest, she would need surgery to have a plate and 12 screws inserted into her arm).

Nancy was charged with three misdemeanors, resisting arrest without violence, trespassing and disorderly intoxication. When the case went to trial, Nancy's attorney introduced the video surveillance from the evening. The film didn't have audio, so there was no way to determine what, if anything, she was saying. But the video did contradict what the police said happened. The video showed Nancy and her husband standing with the officers. Something fell from Nancy's hand and hit the ground. As she bent over to pick it up, police moved in and took her down, breaking her arm.

Regardless of this video, Nancy was found guilty of disorderly conduct, resisting arrest without violence and trespassing. She was sentenced to 360 days probation, a $500 fine and had to write a letter of apology to those she verbally assaulted.

Unfortunately, there isn't a shortage of stories of fights and scuffles at Universal CityWalk. Many seem to be alcohol fueled and the news is peppered with them. Here's an interesting one from October 2013, when a mother and daughter were accused of hitting both an Orlando police officer and a Universal security guard as they left the Groove Dance Club with the daughter's boyfriend. As the boyfriend got into a scuffle with someone he claimed was hitting on his girlfriend, the tag team of mother and daughter had their own melee. Only their fight was allegedly with security and police.

As law enforcement went to clear up the disturbance, all three ended up in a confrontation with authorities. The boyfriend, Aaron, was charged with battery on a security officer. The forty-four-year-old mother, Wanda, was charged with battery on a law enforcement officer and twenty-three-year-old Marissa was charged with battery on a security officer, attempted battery on a law enforcement officer and resisting an officer with violence.

It's not an easy life for a police officer. They truly are some of our country's real life heroes. They tolerate a good deal of undeserved aggression on a daily basis, especially judging by some of the stories featured here. Obviously, there is nothing wrong with a little hero worship when it comes to your local police officers, but sometimes it becomes a little misguided. In August 2013, Christian went to the park for his daughter's sweet sixteen. His attire that day was none other than a t-shirt with the word P O L I C E emblazoned across it.

Officials from Universal spotted him and kicked him out. He offered to buy a new shirt and change but that wouldn't suffice. They booted him from the park anyway. A spokesperson from Universal released the following statement:

"The only people we allow in our parks with shirts or other clothing that might identify themselves as police officers are law enforcement personnel. This is for everyone's safety and to avoid confusion by guests."

Okay, fair enough; don't dress in a shirt an actual police officer may wear on duty. Sounds reasonable and logical. So in this day and age, it probably wouldn't be a great idea to joke about having a bomb in your bag when entering the park either.

Well, this is exactly what happened to forty-five-year-old Sherry visiting from Virginia. As Sherry was trying to enter Universal, a security guard asked her what was in her bag. She quickly closed her bag before security could look inside. When the guard asked again what's in her bag, she smiled and said a bomb.Guess she thought it was funny or cute. In the days of heightened public security, Universal wasn't laughing. They called police; she was arrested and hauled off to jail. The next day she was released on $10,000 bail.

Well, that story concludes the sex and crime blotter for Universal in Orlando. Up next, the accidents and incidents that took place on the attractions themselves. This part of the chapter will only discuss the major accidents. Not the nuisance suits--there was one back in 1998, when a grandmother and her granddaughter sued the park because the haunted house was "too scary" and caused her to slip and fall as she ran for an exit.

When Universal's Islands of Adventure park opened in 1999, an instant favorite among adrenaline junkies and coaster enthusiasts was the Dueling Dragons roller coaster. The inverted ride approaches speeds of 60 miles per hour and has intertwined tracks that feature two ride cars launched simultaneously.

At times, the two cars would pass within 18 inches of each other, giving riders an incredible thrill. By 2010, the ride received a name change and a bit of re-theming to go along with Universal's marketing of Harry Potter.

Today, it is known as the Dragon Challenge. Similar ride but new name. In October of 2011, a minor yet ride-altering tweak was implemented. The dragon would no longer duel; instead the ride was marketed as a chase rather than a duel. The thrilling practice of launching the two coasters simultaneously came to an end.

The reason for the change? More than likely, accidents. The catalyst for the change probably happened the previous summer when two accidents happened within two weeks. The first accident happened to fifty-two-year-old Carlos on vacation from Puerto Rico. Carlos was aboard the ride when something hit him in the face and struck his eye. Already plagued with vision problems in his other eye, this was his "good" eye that he relied on heavily for sight. Tragically, the damage was too severe for physicians to save it and the eye had to be removed. He is now legally blind.

Carlos was riding the coaster in the front row with his wife. At one of the more exhilarating moments of the ride when the dueling coasters intersect and veer extremely close to each other, Carlos felt something strike him in his eye. He immediately began to scream in pain. As soon as the ride ended he was rushed to the hospital.

A similar situation happened roughly two weeks later and again at the same intersection point of the ride. Luckily, the injuries weren't as catastrophic. Nineteen-year-old Jon was on vacation from Ohio and only suffered injuries to his arm, foot and face while aboard the ride. He too was struck by something falling from above.

Park officials speculated that when the two coasters intersect, and one coaster is inverted over the other, items may have been falling out of riders' pockets and causing these freak injuries. Universal noted that over 50 million people have enjoyed the ride since it opened and without prior incident. This doesn't change the situation or bring Carlos his eyesight back.

Moving from one movie franchise to the next, in September of 2003, thirty-four-year-old Leslie was on a three-day work retreat at Universal Studios Orlando for her employer, Godiva Chocolates.

One morning on her trip, Leslie complained that she had pain in her jaw, but other than that it was business as usual. Later that afternoon, she and a few of her colleagues had some free time and headed over to the park. Leslie and her crew went on the Incredible Hulk Coaster at the Islands of Adventure.

The Hulk is two-minute ride that takes park-goers on speeds up to 65 miles an hour, whisks them up a 150-foot tunnel and then spins them into a zero-gravity roll upside down at nearly 100 feet in the air. The coasters strategically-placed cameras catch some of the thrilling experiences aboard the ride. The cameras hope to snap a photo of riders screaming and reacting to the thrills and chills.

On Leslie's ride, the cameras tragically captured Leslie slumped in her seat unconscious. When her ride car pulled into the load area, staff immediately tended to her. They tried CPR and utilized the Automated External Defibrillator on her heart. Paramedics rushed her to the hospital where she was placed in intensive care. Once in the hospital she was unresponsive to commands, and it was determined she had a major heart attack.

According to the hospital's cardiologist, the jaw pain Leslie complained about earlier in the day could have been one of the warning signs of a pending heart attack. Universal shut the ride down after Leslie's incident. The ride was investigated and deemed mechanically sound. Unfortunately, Leslie passed away a few days later in the hospital.

Every amusement park warns visitors about pre-existing health conditions. These conditions could be exasperated by the parks' thrill rides. The warnings implore folks not to take the chance. Tragically, Leslie was most likely unaware of her looming heart condition.

In September of 2004, just a few months after the Revenge of the Mummy ride debuted, thirty-nine-year-old Jose was looking forward to his day at Universal with his wife, Paula. For most of the year, Jose was housebound, awaiting a liver transplant. His wife thought a trip to an amusement park would be a great change for him. They went to the park and Paula carted him around in his wheelchair. Their last stop was a trip on the Revenge of the Mummy Ride. Paula wheeled him to the attraction but decided to sit this one out. She would wait for him until he got off the ride. Jose's journey on the ride was going to be solo.

Unfortunately, Jose didn't even get a chance to ride the

attraction. As he was trying to enter the ride car and take his seat, Jose somehow lost his footing and fell from the loading platform. While he initially survived the four foot fall, he complained of stomach pain and not being able to feel his leg. Jose was rushed to the hospital and underwent surgery to remove his spleen. Days later he passed away of complications from the surgery.

Universal claimed the ride was operating properly and there was no negligence on their part. The medical examiner ruled Jose's death accidental. He died from blunt force trauma to the chest and abdomen. Despite the claim of it being an accident, Jose's wife sued the park for wrongful death. The two sides met with a mediator in April of 2007 and asked for the case to be dismissed; clearly a settlement was reached.

This next incident takes us back, back in time and back to the future. This ride accident happened aboard the Back to the Future ride in January of 2001, when thirty-five-year-old Mary Ann was visiting the park from Louisiana. Mary Ann claimed her trip back to the future was a bumpy one. It was so bumpy and jerky, the movements allegedly gave her a stroke.

If you are unfamiliar, as it closed in 2007, the Back to the Future ride was a simulator-based ride. The technology used for it is based on a modified version of the flight simulators the government and military uses to train pilots. Once aboard the ride, it appears as though you're in motion. In reality, the simulator is playing with your senses. The ride gives the illusion of a tremendous amount of movement, when actually you're not physically moving a great distance at all. The movement is confined to just short intermittent bursts in coordination with a video screen in front of you.

During Mary Ann's ride, she claimed her head was very wobbly. She felt nauseous and knew something was wrong physically. As she walked off the ride, she felt her face go numb, she couldn't speak and she eventually collapsed with right side paralysis. Mary Ann went to the hospital where doctors discovered she had suffered a right side sub arachnoid hemorrhage or stroke.

Universal claimed the ride was in perfect working order. There was nothing mechanically wrong with the ride and up until her complaint there were never any similar accidents or situations. Universal claimed there was no proof the ride caused her stroke. Mary Ann probably takes umbrage with the statements about the ride not causing her stroke. Today, she can speak, walks with a brace and has little use of her right arm. In 2008, after suing the park, both sides reached a confidential out of court settlement.

One of the most horrific Universal Orlando accident stories reportedly happened in early 2014. As the story goes, there was a roller coaster accident and 16 riders were killed. The story swept the world by storm—well, the cyber world at least.

People's Facebook pages were adorned with a story about this tragic accident. In reality, the story was a hoax and another lame attempt to spread spam and a computer virus. Nonetheless, despite the story being a fraud, it did manage to spread across the country and make national news quite quickly.

Another (real) news story making the rounds about Universal in 2014 started back in 2012. Two disabled men sued Universal Hollywood, claiming they were banned from riding a roller coaster because they were handicapped and missing limbs.

Angel, whose forearms were amputated as a child, and Marvin, whose legs were amputated after a car accident, were denied a ride aboard the Revenge of the Mummy roller coaster. The two men claim they rode the ride in prior years, but in 2010, Universal told them they could ride it no longer. The park stated their policies changed and riders must now have at least one arm and one leg. The two men filed a lawsuit in United States District Court and claimed this rule was a violation of the Americans with Disabilities Act (ADA).

In January 2014, the court ruling was handed down. Universal was not in violation of the ADA when it banned the two men. The court said the park wasn't responsible for the ride's design and was within its rights to restrict riders according to manufacturers recommendations. Around the same time Angel and Marvin were filing their lawsuit against Universal, a similar situation played out at Universal's sister park in Orlando.

Seventeen-year-old Katie claimed she was removed from the queue of a roller coaster at Islands of Adventure and denied a ride. Katie was born without hands, and claimed she previously rode coasters at the park. Universal explained their new policy and she wasn't permitted on. Unfortunately for Katie, she experienced a similar situation across town at SeaWorld, which just so happens to be our next stop in Amusement Park 9-1-1.

SEAWORLD

When you think of newsworthy stories involving amusement parks, SeaWorld may not immediately pop into your mind. Sure, they have attractions and rides, their parent company does own Busch Gardens and a few other notable parks (we will get to them in later chapters) but the words SeaWorld and accident usually brings about thoughts of a killer whale story. Entire books and documentaries have been dedicated to SeaWorld's killer whales and what happens to them in captivity. This chapter will focus on that subject as well, but briefly.

In short, there is much more going on at the SeaWorld parks, and it goes beyond freeing Willie. Like Universal Studios, SeaWorld has more than one location. Multiple locations mean more drama, more liability, and more chances for a troubling situation.

Currently, SeaWorld has locations in Orlando, San Diego, and San Antonio and the backstory of a shuttered park in Ohio. Each location has a history of accidents and bizarre incidents. These range from a security guard shooting a park-goer, to a man fatally cutting his toe on a piece of coral, and everything in between.

In the arena of amusement park accidents, sometimes it isn't humans or animals that can create chaos. Often, it is Mother Nature making her presence felt. Florida has the dubious distinction of being the lightning capital of the country—the African country Rwanda owns the title for the world.

In August of 2011, Sea World's Discovery Cove in Orlando felt the wrath of Mother Nature's pop-up thunderstorms. The sister park to SeaWorld features hands on interactions with a variety of marine life. Snorkeling with tropical fish and rays, along with wading in aquatic environments with otters and marmosets are a few of the featured activities. Late one afternoon in August with dark clouds looming, park officials ordered all visitors out of the water and to seek shelter indoors or under cover.

Despite the warnings, many people could not get out of harm's way fast enough. That afternoon, eight people were injured by a lightning strike within the park. In all, three guests and five employees were taken to the hospital. Thankfully, the bolt didn't strike anyone directly, but there were still injuries and a lot of rattled nerves.

Another feature of Discovery Cove is the opportunity to swim and interact with bottlenose dolphins. Sounds like harmless fun, right? Cute little Flipper or his distant cousin has been trained to be polite, playful, and not eat those they are trying to impress. It's the total petting zoo experience in water.

Discovery Cove's showcasing dolphins is another opportunity for SeaWorld to feature something different and interactive in the highly competitive amusement industry. It also becomes another opportunity for accidents to happen, as animal/mammal behavior is often unpredictable despite years of training. Over the years animal unpredictability has made national and international headlines. Siegfried and Roy experienced it with their loyal tigers. In the past, elephants featured in circus acts (and as you will see, amusement parks as well) have been known to crack from the stresses of performing and rampage after anyone near them.

Sea World itself experienced similar negative attention with their killer whale show, and recently with their dolphin attraction. The interactive dolphin attraction at Discovery Cove was plagued with accidental bites from a dolphin, not once but twice over the last few years.

Amusement Park 9-1-1

On November 21, 2012, an eight-year-old girl from Georgia was taking part in an interactive dolphin experience in Orlando. Suddenly, a dolphin lunged up out of the water and bit her. The whole encounter was captured on video and later released on YouTube.

The video shows the young girl standing poolside with countless other children and families. As the dolphins swim up they are hand fed fish from a small white paper plate. Participants are told to keep the paper plate on the ledge in front of them and not in their hands. They are then instructed to pick up the food from the plate and give it to the waiting dolphin. Sounds easy enough.

Well, the little girl made an honest mistake. She picked up her white plate that contained the dolphin's food as the dolphin was in front of her. Within a blink of an eye, the dolphin lunged for the plate, the food and the hand. The dolphin obviously got the food and then some. The little critter punctured the young girls hand in three places. After a few seconds the dolphin released the child's hand, but left her with an unfortunate parting gift.

In February of 2014, this time over at Sea World, San Antonio's Dolphin Cove, a nine-year-old girl's hand was also a snack for a dolphin. The accident happened without a food trigger or catalyst like a white plate filled with fish.

On the young girl's trip to SeaWorld, she was participating in an up close and personal visit with a dolphin. As she reached her hand out to touch the dolphin, it bit her hand and wrist. The dolphin had a strong hold on the girl's arm, so much so, that her mother couldn't get the dolphin to release its grip. Luckily, a park employee was able to free the girl's arm but not without major swelling and bite marks that required medical attention.

When word got out about the incident, a picture shortly

followed (in the day and age of camera phones, very little gets by without being chronicled) and PETA sprung into action (People for the Ethical Treatment of Animals). They demanded the Department of Agriculture investigate this incident via a public statement:

"This incident and exhibit clearly endangered both the dolphin and the public, PETA counsel Brittany Peet said, calling the incident an apparent Animal Welfare Act violation and citing it as just more proof that dolphins shouldn't be confined. It's stressful enough for far-ranging dolphins to be locked up in SeaWorld's tiny tanks, but forcing them to interact with visitors is downright dangerous, said another PETA counselor, Jeff Kerr. SeaWorld's 'Dolphin Cove' is another example of how the park's main priority is profit, not the welfare of the animals or the safety of its guests."

More on PETA and their ongoing battle against SeaWorld to follow, but first a story about a man's battle for his life after cutting his toe in a freak accident at SeaWorld Orlando. In June of 2008, Keith, his wife and two children took a trip across the pond to Central Florida. The family visiting from the United Kingdom spent the day over at Sea World's Discovery Cove. Their day at the cove included a swim in a tropical themed coral reef pool.

While in the pool, fifty-nine-year-old Keith stubbed his toe on a piece of coral. Most would think this bump to the toe would be pretty harmless.

As did Keith, until he reached the airport three days later about to board a plane back to England. At the airport Keith felt ill, he was in agonizing pain and collapsed, his pain was centralized in his shoulder and back. Upon inspection, the skin on his shoulder was completely black, with the coloring continuing down towards his back where it then became a mix of both black and purple.

Keith was immediately taken to a central Florida hospital. His diagnosis was septic shock and organ failure; he was admitted into the intensive care unit in an effort to stabilize him. A few days later his family arranged for him to be transferred back home via air ambulance. Keith was admitted to his local hospital in the U.K., where his condition took a turn for the worse.

Surgeons were forced to amputate his legs below the knee. It appeared as though he contracted Group B streptococcal septicemia, which caused multiple organ failure. The failure resulted in his death on August 8th, roughly eight weeks after his trip to Florida. When the coroner performed the autopsy and spoke with Keith's widow, he informed her, "If ever someone could be described as unlucky, it would be your husband."

Keith was a hemophiliac and otherwise led a pretty normal life physically. Coroner Nigel Meadows had more to say to the widow

"It does seem the most likely source of the infection was the living coral. The presence of tropical fish in the water is always a risk factor with injury because of bugs. This sort of infection, once it grips hold of an individual, can be difficult to treat. Group B streptococcal septicemia is something we can all catch. Some might be more vulnerable to it than others. There might be 100 people who hit coral in the pool. Some people won't pick up the bugs; some people will be more prone. Certainly, his hemophilia would not have helped."

As mentioned earlier, from 1970-2001, SeaWorld owned and operated a park in Aurora, Ohio, roughly 25 miles southeast of Cleveland (the park was sold to Six Flags and then to Cedar Fair Entertainment). SeaWorld Ohio was smaller than the other amusement parks in the SeaWorld family. The park bordered Geauga Lake, and was roughly 50 acres in size and was only open seasonally. In the mid 1990s, the park was looking to capitalize on the popularity of television's Bay Watch (you remember that show. It was known for its tremendous acting from David Hasselhoff and nothing to do with Pamela Anderson in a bathing suit) and featured a 35 minute Bay Watch themed water-ski show.

On August 17, 1996, in front of a capacity crowd of 4,000 people, the show came to a horrifying end. The show was supposed to feature a scene where the driver of the boat leaps from his boat to save someone. As the captain-less boat is charging towards the crowd, at the last moment, it is supposed to veer off to the side and merely splash the crowd with water.

In reality, there obviously is a captain of the boat. He is actually hiding so the crowd can't see him. His job is to commandeer the boat and merely pass by the crowd and give them a quick thrill. Instead, this time the boat didn't veer; it jumped the guardrail and went crashing into the crowd. The 18-foot boat went more than five rows deep into the stands and injured people ranging from two years old to seventy-eight years old.

Most people thankfully only sustained minor injuries. However, seventeen people were taken to the hospital. Four of those transported were in critical condition—the most severe suffered a broken skull. Luckily, none of the injuries were fatal and not more people were injured. When the state investigated the accident it was determined that there were mechanical issues with the boat. In addition, Andrew, the boat's driver, was traveling faster than he should have been. The local municipal court charged him with excessive speeding.

As for the boat's mechanical issues, video of the incident does show Andrew trying to steer the vessel away from the crowd, but to no avail. Upon further investigation of the jet drive, it was determined that it was missing a key component of its steering system.

Unfortunately, the Bay Watch show wasn't SeaWorld's

only boating accident in its history. Ten years prior in 1986, at SeaWorld Orlando, a performer was killed when his Jet Ski crashed into a motorboat in front of 3,000 spectators watching the Ski Pirates Show.

Show performer, twenty-four-year old Tony, had engine trouble with his jet ski and started his routine about 20 seconds late. This was a fatal error as the boating routines were all timed. As Tony drove out from the right side of the grand stand, he was choreographed to use his jet ski to jump over a wake left by a motorboat. That day the wake wasn't there as the show had planned; instead there was a motorboat.

Tragically, Tony crashed into the boat just as it finished its routine and was heading backstage. Crews immediately rescued Tony from the water and rushed him to the hospital. He never regained consciousness and passed away from internal injuries. Tony's parents sued SeaWorld claiming they were at fault for his accident.

In April of 1992, a jury partially sided with Tony's parents. They held Tony 50 percent responsible for the accident and SeaWorld responsible for the other half, as they didn't have appropriate safety procedures in place. They awarded his parents $1.1 million.

There is another case of parents suing SeaWorld after their son perished on the park's property, although this incident is vastly different. This story unfolded back in July of 1999, when Daniel went to SeaWorld in Orlando and lingered around the park after closing. Daniel evaded security and spent the night alone at the park. Long after security was gone, he scaled two fences and made his way towards the 1.5 million gallon tank that housed the largest killer whale in captivity, Tillikum (weighing in at roughly 11,000 pounds).

When park workers arrived the next morning, they found Daniel's partially nude, lifeless body strewn across Tillikum's back. Daniel jumped, fell, or was dragged into the 50-degree water the killer whale inhabited. Daniel's autopsy revealed that he died from hypothermia and drowning—although he did have bruises, bite marks and abrasions throughout his body.

Daniel's parents originally blamed the park for his death. They claimed the park never warned the public that the whale could kill someone. Further, they claimed SeaWorld markets their killer whales as friendly loving creatures and not the violent wild creatures they are. Within a month after the lawsuit was filed they voluntarily withdrew it.

Daniel's story leads us right into the epicenter of just about everything newsworthy and negative about SeaWorld. A quick survey of the Internet or recent news details a growing contingency of people around the country criticizing SeaWorld for the alleged inhumane treatment of their enormous stars. This criticism and strong dislike for the company isn't exclusively from PETA. It seems to be pretty pervasive and has recently intensified after a documentary film titled *Blackfish* debuted.

The documentary touched on the history of SeaWorld and the death of their trainer Dawn, who was killed by Tillikum—who also took Daniel's life. Before Tillikum became the property of SeaWorld and claimed two lives there, the behemoth killed someone while working at Sealand of the Pacific, a public aquarium in Canada.

In 1991, twenty-year-old Keltie was a marine biology student and part-time trainer at Sealand. One day after a killer whale show, Keltie slipped and fell into a tank with 3 killer whales, one of them being Tillikum. The whales kept Keltie submerged, and although she surfaced three times, she was never able to get free and eventually died. After Keltie's death, SeaWorld purchased the three whales and as we know, Tillikum made his way down to Orlando.

Which brings us back to Tillikum, Dawn, *Blackfish* and SeaWorld's current state of affairs. *Blackfish* centers on the controversy or consequences of keeping killer whales in captivity. The documentary claims keeping the whales in captivity is harming them and in turn putting humans, most specifically their trainers, in danger. Case in point would be Dawn's death in February of 2010. Forty-year-old Dawn was a trainer with sixteen years' experience at SeaWorld in Orlando. Her fateful confrontation with Tillikum occurred when the whale surfaced and Dawn started to rub his face after a show titled "Dine with Shamu."

As Dawn showed affection towards Tillikum, he grabbed her by the waist and started thrashing around violently with her in his mouth. In an effort to get the whale to release Dawn, trainers and workers threw nets and food towards him, anything to try and distract him from Dawn. Eventually, he released her but it was too late. The autopsy said she passed away from drowning and blunt force trauma. She suffered a severed spinal cord, broken jawbones, ribs and vertebrae.

After the accident, OSHA conducted a six-month investigation into SeaWorld's practices. They contended that SeaWorld exposed their trainers to unexpected and potentially dangerous incidents involving killer whales at various facilities including their Orlando location. Further, the investigation claimed management failed to make meaningful changes to improve the safety and work environment for its employees. They committed "plain indifference to or intentional disregard for employee safety and health." The report went on to say:

"SeaWorld recognized the inherent risk of allowing trainers to interact with potentially dangerous animals. Nonetheless, it required its employees to work within pool walls, ledges and on shelves where they were subject to dangerous behavior by the animals."

This report was released in August of 2010, along with three citations and a fine of $75,000. In addition to the fine, one of OSHA's citations dealt with the risk the company exposed their trainers to. OSHA recommended that trainers only be allowed to perform with killer whales when protected by physical barriers or sufficient distance. Which obviously means no swimming with them--a major component of their shows.

At the time, SeaWorld said OSHA's claims were unfounded and vowed to fight the accusations and citations. In April of 2014 SeaWorld lost their appeal of the physical barrier recommendation, which would keep the trainers away from the whales. SeaWorld claimed this recommendation was akin to telling the NFL not to allow their players to tackle (with all the concussion news lately, that may not be too far-fetched) or NASCAR to post a speed limit. Each of these fundamentally alters the companies' businesses. Only time will tell if they will appeal this up to the Supreme Court.

Legal wrangling or no legal wrangling, this story is really nothing new. Perhaps only the intense media coverage of it is notable. The stories of animal aggression or animal attacks have been around for years. PETA claims SeaWorld has more than 100 incidents of animal aggression throughout their parks.

These attacks or acts of aggression go all the way back to the early 1970s when the whale that is synonymous with the company, Shamu, had a few incidents. Over the years some of these accidents have even taken their toll on the executive board of the company. Back in 1987 the president of SeaWorld and three other top executives were fired in a shake-up prompted by an accident with a trainer.

An Associated Press story from December of 1987 announced the changes at the top of the corporate ladder. In addition to the departure of the corporate "suits," the company decided to end shows in which killer whales and trainers perform together. This change was prompted by an accident with a twenty-six-

Amusement Park 9-1-1

year-old trainer and the killer whale Orky 2 at SeaWorld San Diego. The trainer, John, had his vertebrae, femur and pelvis crushed, leaving him with permanent injuries.

As history revealed, despite the events of 1987, SeaWorld eventually allowed their trainers to interact with killer whales again, and tragedy struck several more times. But the SeaWorld of yesterday isn't necessarily the same as the SeaWorld of today. As the decades went by, the company changed hands numerous times.

What was created in the 1960s by four friends as an underwater restaurant and entertainment concept, has evolved into what we see today. A quasi-zoo amusement park hybrid, that runs a non-profit with the themes of conservation, education and research interwoven throughout their park and public persona.

Global publisher Harcourt Brace Jovanovich, Anheuser Busch and eventually the current owners, the Blackstone Group, a private equity firm, have owned SeaWorld. In the end, honest intentions aside and public relations wins or losses, it's all about entertainment, making money and turning a profit.

In many folk's eyes the company is immoral and unethical but not necessarily breaking the law. Unfortunately, over the years the same could be said for a few of their employees. Judging by some of their antics, these former SeaWorld employees may have immoral, unethical and felonious already covered.

In May of 2014, thirty-seven-year-old park employee Jimmy Lou was accused of taking money and credit cards from strollers parked in front of Shamu Stadium at SeaWorld Orlando. When a park visitor complained that her purse was missing, security kept a watchful eye over the area. Security then witnessed Jimmy Lou rummaging through bags, purses, and strollers instead of working at the Terrace Garden Food

Buffet.

Although Jimmy Lou didn't take anything on the day they witnessed her handy work. Security did interview her about her actions and she admitted to having a hard time financially. She claimed she was a single mother of three children and did steal money and credit cards on previous occasions.

Jimmy Lou said she took $50 in cash along with multiple credit cards. She claimed she did this so she could buy shoes for her children and gift cards to restaurants so she could feed her family. Jimmy Lou apologized and vowed to pay the money back. SeaWorld escorted her from their property and the Orange County Sheriff's office promptly arrested her and charged her with grand theft. Take-home point: don't take the chance and leave valuables in a stroller. Petty theft stories do happen in the stroller sections in front of rides more often than you think.

Another employee tale of alleged inappropriate behavior happened in March of 2000. In this story, SeaWorld Orlando settled a sexual harassment lawsuit brought forth by three female employees. In 1995, three seasonal underage employees complained to management about a male co-worker who physically touched and made sexually charged comments towards them.

The women's complaints, both verbally and through letters, failed to garner immediate action from management and human resources. After learning of the situation, the United States Equal Employment Opportunity Commission filed a lawsuit on behalf of the trio. Five years later, the case was settled and each woman received $36,000. In addition to making payment, SeaWorld had to implement additional training to their employees about sexual harassment in the work place.

Another sex-related case involving a SeaWorld Orlando worker took place in August of 2010. At the time twenty-four-year-old Brandon was arrested by the FBI for allegedly possessing and distributing child pornography. He was also suspected of engaging in sex with a sixteen-year-old boy.

Brandon graduated from college with a degree in Biology from Bowling Green State University in 2008, and went to work at the park. During the summer of 2010, an FBI undercover online task force began investigating Brandon for utilizing a peer-to-peer file-sharing program. In July, the FBI downloaded sixty child porn images via this file share program. The images were traced back to Brandon's computer. With their evidence in hand, the FBI went to Brandon's house and executed a federal search warrant.

When agents went to work on his computer, they found over 10,000 images and nearly 500 videos of child pornography. Under questioning he admitted to trading in the pornography for over four years. Brandon then admitted to meeting a sixteen-year-old boy online and having a sexual relationship with him. Additionally, he helped another fifteen-year-old boy obtain child pornography by directing him to certain websites that hosted the images. In May of 2011, Brandon was sentenced to seventeen and a half years in federal prison.

This next story is about as disturbing as you can get. The atrocity didn't happen because of a SeaWorld employee, but it was within the confines of the Orlando park.

This horrendous story happened in February of 2011 when twenty-six-year-old Michael went to SeaWorld with his co-worker and the co-worker's family to celebrate the co-worker's birthday. According to the testimony from the trial, when Michael's co-worker wanted to go on a ride with her husband, she asked Michael to watch her two-year-old daughter and five-year-old son for a few minutes while they enjoyed a roller coaster.

While the parents were away, this despicable man molested

the two-year-old girl and photographed the acts with his cell phone. Two days later, Michael's wife found one of the photos on her husband's phone. She contacted the local police department who then came to the home to investigate. Upon searching Michael's computer, they found additional images of child pornography on his hard drive.

When questioned about the photos on his phone and his computer, he denied knowing about them or how they got there. Michael was promptly arrested on charges of sexual battery on a child younger than twelve years old and lewd and lascivious molestation of a child younger than twelve years old. In January of 2012, a federal jury found Michael guilty of sexual exploitation of a child by producing child pornography, distribution of child pornography and possession of child pornography. He was sentenced to thirty years in federal prison.

After news of this story broke, SeaWorld Orlando spokesman Nick Gollattscheck said:

"Nothing is more important than the safety and welfare of our guests, and our team members are trained to report any kind of suspicious behavior. We are cooperating fully with the Orange County Sherriff's office investigation. Illegal behavior of any type is not tolerated at our parks. Our thoughts are with the family at this very difficult time."

The safety and security of the public should certainly be priority number one for all amusement park operators. Especially with the climate of our country's post 9/11 era and the era of frequent mass public shootings. Thankfully, most amusement parks (and their guests) haven't faced many violent public displays of aggression that led to catastrophic situations. There were notable stories of violence at Universal CityWalk and in the next chapter we will discuss a few more violent outbreaks at Six Flags. But before we get there, believe it or not, SeaWorld in San Diego had an incident that escalated into a shooting.

Amusement Park 9-1-1

Back in October of 1979, thirty-one-year-old Larry began shouting incoherently and acting odd around visitors and workers. Two security guards approached Larry and asked him to leave the grounds. If he would leave they would go ahead and refund his ticket. Larry refused the refund and became more erratic and wild. The guards got closer to Larry and tried to escort him off the property. At which point, he asked the guards, "Have you ever heard of plastic explosives? I'm going to blow you guys up."

The guards then tried to restrain Larry physically. As they did this, Larry looked as though he was reaching towards his belt with his free hand. In reaction, one of the security guards pulled out a .38 caliber pistol and shot Larry in the shoulder. He survived the shooting, and the police deemed the guard's reaction justifiable.

Despite these incidents, the SeaWorld parks have basically been violence-free when it comes to person-on-person violence. But as we know, the future is filled with uncertainty, especially when it comes to violence on the macro scale or in regards to terrorism.

In 2008 the United States Department of Homeland Security (DHS) reached out to SeaWorld about the possibility of their parks becoming a target for terrorists. In 2007, the DHS developed new regulations regarding universities, research facilities and businesses that work with chemicals that could be lucrative targets for terrorists to steal and use in an attack.

These regulations fell under the Chemical Facility Anti-Terrorism Standards Act. The act identified a list of 300 chemicals the government declared dangerous in the wrong hands. Facilities possessing large stockpiles of chemicals on the list had to submit their inventory of substances to the government for review. SeaWorld caught the attention of the DHS, since they deal in large amounts of chlorine and other chemicals used at their parks. SeaWorld complied and provided the DHS with any necessary information to keep their park and the public safe.

Well, this wraps up the scandals and situations at SeaWorld. Up next is Six Flags. Get ready for an action-packed chapter. Six Flags has numerous parks across the country with tens of millions of visits over the years.

As you're about to read, many of those visits started out as just another day at an amusement park looking for some fun. Tragically they ended up differently.

SIX FLAGS

The Six Flags Entertainment Corporation originated in Texas during the early 1960s. Today, the company is the world's largest amusement corporation based on their number of locations scattered throughout North America. Number of locations aside, Six Flags is collectively the fifth most popular amusement destination based on attendance figures from 2013. Across their brand their annual attendance hovers in the neighborhood of 25 million people a year. In comparison, Disney, the obvious leader in the industry, has annual attendance figures closer to 130 million people.

As of 2014, Six Flags has a presence in nine states. Over the years the company has become an amalgamation of sorts. They've built their own parks, purchased existing ones and even sold or closed a few. Unfortunately, a common thread throughout their properties is the cornucopia of tragedy that spans decades.

With Six Flags having the largest amusement park presence based on number of locations in the U.S., Canada and Mexico, it is no surprise the company is the majority owner of roller coasters in North America. Most of Six Flags' coasters soar way over fifty feet tall and travel at speeds north of 50 miles per hour. These facts may also lead to the dubious distinction of having some of the most horrifying and gruesome amusement park deaths on record.

As reiterated over the past few chapters, accidents aren't an everyday occurrence at amusement parks. However, when they do happen, they obviously catch people off guard, make front-page news and leave people maimed or dead.

As mentioned in the introduction, the federal government doesn't regulate or inspect permanent amusement parks. Also noted was federal legislation that failed to pass in 2007 and 2011.Two decades prior, the same thing happened back in 1985 when the U.S. House of Representatives was looking to exercise some control over the industry. The bill from 1985 gained attention after a fire killed eight people at Six Flags in New Jersey—sit tight for that story, it's coming up soon.

When each government proposal came up, Six Flags and the other permanent parks have (and will most likely always) opposed federal oversight and inspections. The consensus is federal inspections wouldn't necessarily prevent mishaps. The industry claims they are diligent on their own and go through their own safety inspections. Any government involvement would lead to more costs for the parks.

Back in 2003, Six Flags was proactive and showed some diligence when they orchestrated a brain injury study concerning roller coaster rides and traumatic brain injury. After feeling the pressure of negative publicity about ride safety at Six Flags, the company reached out to the American Association of Neurological Surgeons and an engineering firm, Exponent Failure Analysis, to conduct a study.

The two groups examined eighty brain-injury cases that were an alleged result of a roller coaster ride. Of these cases, only the violent motion of a roller coaster could have caused nine of the head injuries. Yet even with these nine cases, the study couldn't be totally conclusive as to the exact cause. Thus the two groups concluded that there is no correlation with roller coasters and brain injury. Six Flags released their study with a definitive, "the rides are safe."

Several of the incidents featured in this book and chapter may have you thinking otherwise about that research. Here it is, a park-by-park look at Six Flags and the accidental, incidental or criminal events that unfolded on their properties.

Six Flags Over Texas: Arlington, Texas

Beginning with one of the more recent and tragic accidents first, let's take a trip down to Texas. Six Flags Over Texas is the amusement park that started it all for the Six Flags Company. The park debuted in 1961 and has been a staple in the company's portfolio ever since. In March of 1990, the park premiered the world's tallest wooden roller coaster, The Texas Giant.

In 2011 the ride was refurbished, redesigned and reopened for the park's fiftieth anniversary celebration. The coaster is now dubbed The New Texas Giant and is the tallest wooden steel hybrid coaster in the world. The refurbishment added a new steel track and featured a record-breaking 95-degree bank and 79-degree drop. Both of these are records for any other wooden coaster.

On July 19, 2013, The New Texas Giant was the scene for an awful tragedy. Fifty-two-year-old Rosa was visiting the park with her family. Rosa, her daughter and son-in-law decided to take a trip aboard the coaster.

As the family was seated into the ride, there was some uncertainty as to whether Rosa's harness locked all the way down or if the safety mechanism was faulty. According to the police report and court documents, Rosa inquired if her harness was secure. She was informed it was. The ride's computer recognized her harness was down far enough and that it was locked; all systems were go. All clear, and off the coaster went. Rosa's daughter and her husband were riding in the car immediately in front her, Rosa was riding solo. Shortly after the ride pulled out of the loading platform, Rosa's daughter looked behind and heard her mother screaming. She was practically upside down in her car with her head on the floor and feet dangling out of the car.

Nearby passengers tried in earnest to grab Rosa's legs and

help her, but they were unable to do so. As the ride made its third ascent twisting and turning, tragedy struck. Rosa's daughter watched in horror as her mother was tossed from the ride car at a height of over 75 feet. After being ejected, it took rescuers over an hour to find Rosa. She was nearly severed in half with her body wrapped around one of the ride support beams. She was lying on top of the roof of the Honky Tonk tunnel, which covers the lower portion of the ride.

Needless to say, Rosa didn't survive this accident and her family filed a lawsuit against the park. In October of 2013, Six Flags denied that they were responsible for her death as they were not the manufacturer of the coaster. They indicated that over 2.5 million people rode the coaster before the accident, all without serious incident.

Six Flags closed the attraction for two months due to the accident's investigation. When it reopened, a few safety changes were made. The New Texas Giant featured new seat belts and a redesigned restraint bar pad. Oh yeah, remember that blurb about Rosa's inquiry to the ride operators about her harness being fully engaged? Well, according to the Arlington Police report, the ride operator (who was relatively new to his position) told investigators he checked everyone's restraints before the train departed, but when the coaster went by, he remembered thinking the restraint wasn't all the way down on Rosa's thigh. The family's lawsuit is still pending.

Regrettably, Rosa's death wasn't the only one on site at Six Flags over Texas. Back in March of 1999, twenty-eight-year-old Valeria was visiting the park with friends and family from Arkansas. Valeria and her crew descended on the Roaring Rapids ride for some simulated white water rafting.

The rapids ride debuted in 1983, and takes up to 12 people in an inflatable circular raft through a cascading and often turbulent waterway that is two-to-three-feet deep. A few feet of water doesn't sound too daunting.

Amusement Park 9-1-1

Well, a high-stakes emergency situation revealed just how daunting and tragic this situation can be when a trip goes awry. On Valeria's fateful journey everything seemed to be going well on her simulated trip down the rapids. However, just 200 feet before the end of the ride and unbeknownst to the passengers of the raft, the boat was deflating. As it deflated, it started to take in water. Suddenly. the raft flipped over and trapped Valeria underneath it, keeping her submerged in the water.

All of the passengers (Valeria's brother included) were able to unfasten their safety belts and get free either by themselves or with help from other guests watching in horror. Valeria was not able to get free; she was pinned underneath the boat and submerged in the water where she tragically drowned.

Shockingly, from an Associated Press article about the accident just days later on March 24, 1999, the article writer interviewed witnesses to the accident and claimed the workers from Six Flags stood by and watched as the raft's riders struggled for their lives. Not only did they not offer assistance, some claimed the workers implored other guests not to go into the water and help rescue the trapped passengers.
The employees working the attraction allegedly told park visitors-turned-future-heroes to sit tight, while they activated an emergency system, which called in paramedics. Thankfully, some of the guests didn't listen, most notably, a certified scuba diver waiting to board the ride. This good person was able to help save several passengers.

Valeria's family sued Six Flags and the above-mentioned story was one of the hallmarks of their case. The other component of the lawsuit dealt with the raft itself. It appears as though the raft snagged a pipe on the bottom of the waterway causing the air bladders to deflate. In 2002, her family settled their lawsuit against Six Flags. The family received $4 million, which was put into a trust for Valeria's young daughter.

Six Flags' troubles in Texas didn't end with Rosa and Valeria's deaths (they were the only two deaths at Six Flags' flagship park in nearly 60 years in business). Across the state in San Antonio, Six Flags Fiesta Texas had a few incidents as well.

Six Flags Fiesta Texas: San Antonio

On a hot summer day in June of 2007, fourteen-year-old Hailey was standing in the queue for the roller coaster, the Poltergeist. The Poltergeist features four inversions, travels at speeds close to 60 miles an hour and pulls over 4g's (4 times the force of gravity pushing down on your body).

Sadly, Hailey would never experience the thrill and adrenaline rush of this coaster. As she was waiting to board on the ride platform, she fainted and fell through the space between the roller coaster cars. Unlike many other coasters across the country that are equipped with netting or safety systems underneath, Poltergeist's was not. The only thing below Hailey was concrete. Young Hailey fell ten feet and landed on the ground below the coaster, leaving her paralyzed.

Six years later, also in June, something much different but nonetheless disturbing and unsettling happened at the park. Thankfully the child involved wasn't paralyzed or killed. They were however, robbed of their innocence and subjected to the perversions of a thirty-nine-year-old man.

A thirteen-year-old girl was enjoying the day with her family at Fiesta Texas' water park. While off swimming away from her parents, she noticed a man smiling at her. Feeling uncomfortable, she started to walk back to her parents. The man started to pursue her, and before she could reach her family, Jose reached out and allegedly molested her. Once she was able to get free, the young girl made it back to her family and was able to point out the man to her father.

Her father grabbed the man and waited for security to come. Jose was arrested and charged with indecency with a child.

Six Flags AstroWorld: Houston, Texas (1968-2005)

The last two stories in Texas took place at what is now a parking lot. Six Flags AstroWorld was a seasonal amusement park located in Houston. The park was in existence from 1968 to 2005. In 2005, its demise was attributed to a few things; most notably its performance and location near the Houston Texans football stadium.

Before the park's demolition, it was the scene of a gruesome accident for a thirteen-year-old boy in the summer of 2001. Sam loved roller coasters and amusement parks, as so many folks do. The young man was proud of his season pass to the park and used it several times a week.

One evening Sam headed over to The Mayan Mindbender. He went aboard the ride four times consecutively, just before the park was closing. With still a few minutes of time left before the park was set to close, Sam was able to sneak in one more trip on the Mayan-themed twisting roller coaster (it has since been re-named and re-themed the Hornet and resides at Wonderland in Amarillo), making it a total of five rides in succession

On his last trek, Sam got a seat in the coveted first car of the ride, and his pal John climbed in behind him. The two boys were off, and excitedly, John clutched Sam's shirt anticipating the thrills and chills of the ride. As the ride ascended three stories, Sam raised his arms, the coaster veered and dipped as it did millions of times before. Then something happened that hadn't happened previously. Sam was thrown from the car and went flying off the ride and crashed into the concrete below. Sam broke every bone in his face. The force of impact also splintered his hip, snapped his pelvis, fractured his ankle and a piece of bone was lodged into his brain. He was rushed to the hospital where he continued to have trouble breathing as blood had filled his airway. Once in the hospital, Sam's face had to be surgically peeled away ear to ear and chin to scalp, so surgeons could reconstruct his face. Recovery was slow and it took Sam two months to open his eyes. By the third month, he could be discharged.

Sam's family sued the park after the accident. Six Flags defense was Sam didn't follow the park's rules. Had he followed them, he wouldn't have fallen off. When Sam was lying mangled in blood on the concrete, a Six Flags worker began to question him as to what happened.

He told her he was "jumping up and down on his seat." This quote became the park's defense at the trial. Sam later in court claimed he never said those words. Sam's legal team investigated the ride's history and maintenance records. It appeared as though the common T-bar type restraint used across many coasters, and specifically for the Mayan Mindbender, was known to have problems.

In addition, just one week before Sam's accident, maintenance records showed issues with the ride's T-bars. Three days before Sam's accident the ride was even shut down briefly for this problem. The revelation of these issues damaged Six Flags' case, and the two parties reached a $1.7 million settlement. Unfortunately, Sam still has cognitive deficits and suffered from posttraumatic stress disorder as a result of the accident. Physically, he still has numerous scars and difficulty breathing through his nose.

The last accident at AstroWorld took place on a school trip in 2000. Patty was a cosmetology teacher in her early 40s. She was all about her students (as you will come to see) and seeing them through their graduation celebrations. Patty joyfully followed "her kids" throughout the park and shared in their end of the school year festivities.

Patty and the students headed over to the Dungeon Drop around 10:30 at night. This ride features a tower that lifts riders into the air and then drops them into a somewhat controlled free fall. That evening, as with most evenings, the attraction brought riders to the apex of the attraction and dropped them, 62 miles an hour in 3 seconds. Then the ride's breaking mechanism kicks in and brings the ride to a stop.

Patty plunged quickly, as did everyone. However, Patty's body responded differently than her fellow riders did. When the ride came to an abrupt stop after the plunge, her stomach lining ripped and bulged into her belly button. As she stepped off the ride, she couldn't stand completely upright without intense pain. Despite the pain she still had to watch over her students. She spent the next two hours writhing in pain on a park bench waiting for the evening to end—what a dedicated teacher!

The next day, Patty went to the hospital. She had an epigastria hernia and received 8 staples and 39 internal stitches to fix her problem. Patty eventually sued the park, and after two years of a legal tug of war, she settled for $12,000.

Six Flags Great Adventure: Jackson, New Jersey

Long before MTV made riveting and captivating television with their show *Jersey Shore* (sarcasm detector working?), a mere 30 miles to the west, Six Flags Great Adventure has been producing their own drama since 1974, in Jackson, New Jersey.

The seasonally operated park in the Garden State draws crowds from both the New York City and Philadelphia metropolitan areas, as it is situated between both of these cities. Great Adventure is one of the largest amusement parks in the country and boasts some of the fastest and highest coasters in the world.

Since it debuted, the park has become much more than a day out for adrenaline junkies, but a day that could include a trip to a water park, a trek through a wildlife safari and from time to time, an accident.

This book isn't about quantifying which amusement park is the deadliest. Nor is it an effort to scare you into not enjoying yourself on a ride or two (although, I must admit after doing the research for the book, I would be lying if I didn't say it hasn't affected my views somewhat). With that being said, Six Flags Great Adventure has certainly seen its share of horrible events over the years.

The 1980s saw the lion's share of trouble for Great Adventure. It all started with an accidental death of an employee in 1981. The death happened on one of the mainstays of the park at the time, the coaster Rolling Thunder. This wooden coaster had speeds reaching roughly 55 miles per hour and featured an 85-foot drop. The coaster debuted in 1979 and just two short years later it claimed the life of a park employee.

On the morning of August 16, 1981, Scott, a twenty-year-old employee, was giving the coaster a test ride. During Scott's fateful ride, he was thrown over 40 feet from the coaster and was killed. The ride was immediately closed and inspected both by Six Flags and OSHA. The investigation revealed no mechanical problems or issues with the ride. Officials estimated the coaster was traveling around 35 miles per hour when Scott was ejected. Investigators determined that Scott didn't put the ride's safety bar down before his test run started. An autopsy revealed Scott died of a fractured skull and other internal injuries. OSHA cited the park for Scott's death.

Two weeks later, on August 29th, eighteen-year-old Colleen also died after riding Rolling Thunder. In another freak accident, Colleen had just finished dinner before boarding the roller coaster. When the coaster pulled back in to the platform, Colleen was choking and having trouble breathing. She was rushed to the hospital where she passed away. Colleen's death was described as aspiration of gastric contents; she essentially choked to death.

Just a year before the debut of Rolling Thunder, Great Adventure premiered a Haunted Castle for guests to explore in 1978. Several years later this attraction would be the scene of one of the more tragic and deadly amusement park accidents in history.

When the Haunted Castle opened, it was crafted from four aluminum tractor-trailers, exactly like the ones seen hauling goods on just about every highway in this country. A year later, due to the attraction's success, the attraction was expanded to a total of 17 interconnected trailers. The trailer-to-trailer connections were made via wood, plaster, foam pads and rubber. This assembly created a labyrinth of walkways for visitors to traverse.

The castle was a popular walk-through attraction that tried to scare everyone who entered. It featured a spooky setting with creepy strobe lights, music and monsters lurking in the shadows waiting to startle and scare everyone who enters—a rat lady and a hunchback were a couple of the creatures looming inside.

One Friday night, this make-believe haunted house turned into a real life house of horrors. On May 11, 1984, roughly thirty people including employees were inside the Haunted Castle when it caught on fire. Even as the fire burned guests were still being allowed to enter the attraction. One guest recounted that as she weaved in and out of the very dark and misleading corridors, she saw flames. Initially, she thought they were part of the attraction. As she got closer and smelled the smoke she exited as quickly as possible.

While she and many others were able to make their way out, eight teenagers were unable to escape and perished inside. At the time, a volunteer firefighter at the scene recalled not being able to distinguish the prop skeletons of the attraction from the unfortunate teens that were burnt so badly. Some victims' remains had to be identified via dental records.

Tragically, the castle featured no sprinkler system or smoke detectors. It wasn't even inspected by the township's building inspector. The materials used to connect the trailers and line the walls (foam and wood) caught fire quickly and engulfed the entire attraction in roughly three and a half minutes.

After the fire and the revelation of no sprinklers or inspection, the park and two park managers were charged by the state of New Jersey with aggravated manslaughter. The charges included "reckless conduct amounting to extreme indifference to human life for failing to take adequate fire prevention measures."

After an 8-week trial and 13 hours of deliberation the jury sent back a non-guilty verdict for the company, despite some damning testimony from employees. Some of the castle's employees testified that they often complained to management about the dangers of the attraction.

A major complaint was the attraction was too dark. Often when employees would pop out to scare a visitor, the visitors were so frightened they would try and run out of the castle. This led to broken ankles and teeth from falling or crashing into the walls. As for the two park managers charged, they avoided a trial by agreeing to lengthy community service programs.

In the end it was actually something the park installed for safety that was a major propellant for the blaze. Along the walls, padding was installed in case visitors bumped into them. That evening, a fourteen-year-old boy was trying to find his way out and used his lighter to illuminate his path. He accidentally bumped into a polyurethane-lined wall and set it on fire. He attempted to put it out with his hands but was unable to do so. He continued to walk through the castle and didn't notify anyone of his actions.

After the heartbreak for these families, and the park's drop in attendance, Six Flags announced that $5.2 million worth of sprinklers and computerized smoke and heat detectors would be installed in all their enclosed attractions.

As previously mentioned, the 1980s were tough years for Great Adventure. After the horrors of the Haunted Castle, the park had a bit of a reprieve. Then 1987 rolled around and the park was the setting for a shooting, two stabbings, animal attack and a death after a young girl fell from a roller coaster.

The evening of April 19th, 1987 was an extraordinarily violent night for any amusement park. Every park has seen their share of scuffles or squabbles over cutting in line or petty disagreements. Often this is what happens when large groups of people get together.

On this Easter Sunday at Great Adventure things surpassed disagreements and escalated into shooting and stabbing. The three separate incidents led to the park closing early that evening. The first incident happened around 4:30 at an arcade, when a seventeen-year-old girl stabbed a seventeen-year-old boy in the neck. The young man was taken to the hospital, and the young lady was arrested and charged with aggravated assault. This stabbing was an attempt to steal two gold rings from the teen.

An hour later at the park's entrance, two eighteen-year-old men got into an argument. The argument evolved into an altercation when one man was stabbed repeatedly by the other. Same outcome here-- one got a trip to the hospital, the other to jail.

About an hour and half later, just before 7:00 P.M., with the park's occupancy in the neighborhood of 22,000 people, a man standing at the Liberty Fountain near the main gate of the park pulled out a chrome plated revolver and started randomly shooting into the crowd. The crowd panicked and chaos ensued. A twenty-three-year-old man, Anthony, was hit in the arm and leg, two wounds he thankfully survived. The shooter escaped through the crowd and exited the park.

This day of violence led to many changes at the park. Metal detectors were installed, sales of beer and wine were halted and all visitors had to wear shirts and shoes. These moves were made in an effort to bring back a family atmosphere.

The incidents that season only got worse with a fatality. On June 17th, nineteen-year-old Karen plunged to her death during her ride on the Lightnin Loops roller coaster. The ride debuted at the park in 1978 and featured two 85-foot tall 360-degree loops. When Karen boarded the ride with her boyfriend, they sat in the last car. Tragically, she wasn't properly secured in her shoulder harness when the coaster took off.

When the coaster made its way out of the loading area and down the hill on its initial run, Karen was thrown 75 feet. She was pronounced dead at the hospital from skull fractures. Upon investigating the ride, the state found it was operating properly, but her death was a result of operator error. The ride operator didn't follow proper procedures and should have made sure the safety harnesses secured all the passengers. The park was charged the maximum state fine for this violation, $1,000.

The last accident from the 1980s also happened in 1987, when a camel from the park's safari attacked a handler. Thirty-two-year-old Susan was a gatekeeper at the park's safari. Her job description is as her job title declares. She opens the gate or closes it when the animals need to make their way through different areas of the attraction.

On the fourth of July, an eleven-year-old female camel got aggressive with Susan. She bit her, knocked her over and then sat on top of her, breaking Susan's back. Susan's back was so badly fractured she was hospitalized for several weeks and underwent surgery for her injuries, eventually spending weeks in a body cast.

When OSHA investigated the incident they noted Susan didn't have any forms of communication to radio someone for help. The park was fined for improper training, hazardous work conditions and lack of adequate equipment—they said the park didn't have *enough* whips, poles or electric prods for employees. Susan filed a lawsuit against the park, which was eventually settled out of court.

Animal accidents at Great Adventure aren't exclusive to the safari attraction. In July of 2012, twelve- year-old Shane was involved in an animal accident of his own while he was riding the world's tallest and fastest roller coaster, Kingda Ka.

Standing at 456 feet tall and launching riders at speeds near 130 miles per hour in roughly three and a half seconds, the attraction is amazing. As you can imagine, everything on the ride happens very fast. So fast, that one day when Shane was enjoying the ride he was struck in the face by a passing bird. In the freak accident, Shane was riding in the front car and as the coaster approached the station, something hit his face. He wondered what happened. Did someone throw something?

As he began to spit out feathers and noticed the blood all over, he knew it was a bird. Luckily for Shane, he only suffered some bruising. The same couldn't be said for the bird. The little critter basically exploded on impact. A similar situation happened back in 1999 at Busch Gardens with everyone's favorite male model and former butter "pitchman." Sit tight for that one; Busch Gardens is the next chapter.

This wraps up Six Flags Great Adventure in New Jersey. Next stop is a trip down the east coast and to Six Flags Over Georgia, located just outside of Atlanta.

Kermit Gonzalo

Six Flags Over Georgia: Austell, Georgia

With the success of Six Flags Over Texas, the company sought to replicate their park a few states over in Georgia. Six Flags Over Georgia, located just outside of Atlanta, debuted in June of 1967. Today, the park features over 40 attractions and nearly a dozen coasters.

One of those coasters is the very popular Batman: The Ride. This coaster is a hallmark of the Six Flags franchise as it can be enjoyed in a half a dozen of their parks. Batman is an inverted steel coaster that features a 360-degree loop and a zero-g roll at speeds approaching 50 miles per hour. It surely gets the riders' adrenaline going.

Sadly, the ride has taken two lives, neither of which happened while aboard the coaster. Both deaths were similar in nature and most likely could have been prevented if the victims thought a bit more about their actions before they acted. In 2002 just five years after the ride opened a fifty-eight-year-old groundskeeper, Samuel, was killed when he walked under a restricted and locked area beneath the coaster.

As Samuel stood in the prohibited area, he was struck in the head by a fourteen-year-old girl's leg as her ride car passed by. The young girl injured her leg and was taken to the hospital where she was eventually released. Samuel wasn't as fortunate; tragically he passed away from traumatic head injuries.

Six years later in June of 2008, a similar scenario played out when a teenager was decapitated as the ride passed over him. He too stood in the unauthorized area, as the ride flew by at nearly 50 miles per hour. Just minutes before his death, seventeen-year-old Asia took a ride on Batman. During his ride his hat flew off. Determined to get it back, Asia ignored the warning signs, scaled 2 six-foot fences, and entered the restricted area to fetch his hat.

Amusement Park 9-1-1

At this time, the ride fatally struck him— a similar scenario played out two months later in August 2008 across the country at Six Flags Magic Mountain when the coaster Ninja also struck a person after trying to retrieve their hat.

High blood pressure, heart issues, back problems, there are a litany of conditions that may be exasperated by taking a ride on a coaster. As this book will reveal all too often, it appears so many folks don't realize they have a pre-existing condition and board a roller coaster. Some live to tell about their ride, others aren't as fortunate and succumb to their unknown health problems.

In July of 2006, a forty-five-year-old man boarded the Goliath roller coaster with its 175-foot drop and blazing speeds of 70 miles per hour. The man was conscious and alert as the ride started. By the end of the ride, when the coaster pulled back into the loading area, he was unconscious and not breathing. Paramedics arrived on the scene and transported him to the hospital where he was pronounced dead. His cause of death was a heart attack.

The last accidental death aboard a ride at Six Flags Over Georgia took place in July of 1989 when an eleven-year-old boy was found unconscious in his seat after riding the roller coaster Z-Force.

The steel coaster was only onsite at the park for two years, 1988-1990. Then it was relocated to Magic Mountain in California. Tragically, the year before it was relocated, William died after his trip on the ride. As with so many of these stories, the boy entered the ride with his family and felt fine. By the time the ride was over, disaster had already struck. In William's case the medical examiner said the boy suffered a seizure-like episode. This episode may have been exasperated by the ride's acceleration or G-forces, as these things may have lowered the boy's seizure threshold.

Kermit Gonzalo

Six Flags Great Adventure wasn't the only park in the corporation to be the scene of some unsavory behavior. Here are a few more stories from Georgia to add to the collection of larcenous, violent and sexually corrupt behavior.

These next two stories, while not entirely on Six Flags property, did directly involve the park. Either the drama started at the park and spilled out elsewhere or involved park employees, or both. The first situation happened when a dispute between two men inside the park escalated outside of it.

In July of 2006, two men got into an argument inside the park. Eventually, they were separated and went on their separate ways. The two men reconvened at a bus stop adjacent to the park. One man was waiting for the bus, the other pulled up to the stop in his car. Reunited for the wrong reasons, the two men began exchanging words. The man driving the car pulled out a gun and began firing at the bus stop. The shots hit two adults and a teenager; all three of them survived the shooting.

A year later, same month, also at the bus stop adjacent to the park, a terrible random crime happened. Nineteen-year-old Joshua was waiting at the stop with his brother and a friend after their day at Six Flags. The three guys were celebrating an acceptance to college. As the trio waited for the bus, they were approached by a gang of men (literally, they were apart of the YGL, Young Gangster Living). A few of the gang members were also Six Flags park employees.

For whatever reason, the gang was looking for a fight that day. These "tough guys" were initially heckling a family in the park but security stepped in and broke it up. Unsuccessful on their initial attempt to rumble, the gang decided they would beat the man up later when he exited the park. This plan changed as they were leaving Six Flags and came across Joshua.

For no rhyme or reason the gang approached Joshua and

Amusement Park 9-1-1

his companions, and they proceeded to beat them unmercifully. All three men were injured but none as severe as Joshua. He received multiple blows and kicks to the head (there was actually a sneaker sole imprint on his head) and countless punches to the body, head and face with brass knuckles.

The thugs eventually fled the scene and got away on a public bus, Joshua left in an ambulance. The beating put him in a coma for a week with a traumatic brain injury. As a result, he now suffers from permanent brain damage. Joshua eventually recovered, he still has cognitive and speech issues and will require therapy and care for the rest of his life. He filed suit against Six Flags, and in November 2013 was awarded $35 million. The park was deemed 92% at fault; the thugs that beat Joshua were accountable for the rest.

Deandre, Brad, Claude and Willie were the teens involved. They were all charged with aggravated battery and violation of the Georgia gang act, both felonies. Police also charged them with two misdemeanors, battery and simple assault. In addition to being held responsible for a percent of the damages, each received time in prison. Brad, Claude and Willie were employees of the park.

The last two stories took place at Six Flags Over Georgia's White Water Park. In June 2012, a couple of knuckleheads made some waves of their own at the water park, a crime wave. Twenty-seven-year-old Amanda and eighteen-year-old Xavier allegedly stole cash, credit cards and any other valuables they could get their hands on. The theft took place when trusting park-goers left their bags unattended while they enjoyed the park.

Over a three-day period the cousins hit ten victims and pilfered nearly $3,000 by using the stolen debit and credit cards at a local Wal-Mart. Police, Wal-Mart security and Six Flags security all worked together to apprehend the duo. The two criminal masterminds grabbed the credit cards and took a stroll over to Wal-Mart, where they loaded their shopping carts with big-ticket items. After they purchased the items they resold them at a discounted price. The cousins were apprehended and charged with 12 felony counts of theft by taking and credit card fraud.

Sadly, the last story is also about stealing. Again, about stealing young children's innocence. In June of 2013, convicted rapist and sex offender Kenyon was arrested for allegedly molesting two young girls at the park. The girls, ages thirteen and fifteen, were in line for a water ride when Kenyon pushed his pelvis and genitals against the buttocks of the thirteen-year-old girl.

In the other deplorable act, Kenyon touched the fifteen-year-old girl between her legs while she too waited in line. The two young girls immediately told their family members who informed security and brought the authorities in. Kenyon was arrested on charges of two accounts of child molestation.

This closes out Six Flags Over Georgia. Our next stop takes us over to the "Big Easy" and to a park that is now just a memory.

Six Flags New Orleans (2003-2005)

Everyone knows what happened in New Orleans during August of 2005. One of the deadliest hurricanes in United States history hammered the city leaving a trail of death and destruction.

One of the casualties of Hurricane Katrina was Six Flags New Orleans. Six Flags took over the amusement park originally known as Jazzland in 2003. Just two years into their ownership the park was closed due to the devastation brought by the hurricane (Six Flags got out of their 75 year lease with the city in 2009).

Amusement Park 9-1-1

Despite being open a mere two years, the park was the scene of a deadly accident in July 2003. Fifty-two-year-old Rosa decided to take an impromptu trip to the park with her four-year-old grandson D'Kota. Once in the park, Rosa and D'Kota headed over to the Jokers Jukebox. The "Joker" had six mechanical arms with five cars on each arm that spin independently. In addition to spinning, they go up and down. In the industry, it's considered a "round thrill ride."

That Wednesday evening in July, Rosa was working to secure D'Kota into the attraction when the operator accidentally started the ride. Tragically, one of the ride's spinning cars hit Rosa in the head. A second car came by and struck her in the abdomen. Paramedics were called to the scene but Rosa couldn't be saved. She passed away before she was able to get to the hospital. The coroner said she died from blunt force trauma and a crushed pelvis. Her death was ruled accidental.

Six Flags immediately closed the ride for an investigation, and they determined it was mechanically sound. The bigger question from the investigation was why was Rosa allowed to be so close to the ride, and why didn't the ride operator notice her?

A week after the accident the ride reopened with new safety features. Two convex mirrors, 3 feet across, were mounted at a 45-degree angle adjacent to the ride operator's station. This allowed the operators to see all of the cars and the spaces between them. A public address system also began to broadcast instructions for loading and unloading cars.

As a Six Flags spokesperson said, "The changes should not be taken to indicate that the Joker's Jukebox ride was unsafe before Rosa's death Wednesday," said Ann Wills, spokeswoman for Six Flags New Orleans. "These tools are being implemented solely to give the ride operator an additional level of confidence."

Kermit Gonzalo

Six Flags Kentucky Kingdom (1998-2010)

For more than a decade, what is now known as Kentucky Kingdom was known as Six Flags Kentucky Kingdom. Since its inception in 1987, the park's ownership has changed hands several times. While each ownership group faced their share of adversity from declining attendance and accidents, no owner faced the horrifying accident and subsequent national news headlines like Six Flags faced when they owned the park until 2010.

Just like Six Flags Over Georgia and their Batman coaster, superhero-themed rides dominate Six Flags parks. One of these popular attractions was the Superman Tower of Power ride that resided at Six Flags Kentucky Kingdom.

This thrill ride is an enormous free fall ride. Riders are fastened into their seats in a ride car that is attached to a nearly 200-foot tower. The cars then ascend up the tower at about 10 miles an hour. They level off at around 177 feet where they pause momentarily.

After the slight pause they are dropped over 150 feet at a speed of nearly 55 miles an hour. Finally, the brakes kick-in and the ride comes to a stop about 20 feet above the ground. The riders then slowly make their way back down to ground level. Sounds like an exhilarating ride aboard Superman. However, the ride wasn't always known as the man of steel. Until 2007, the ride was actually called the Hellavator.

A ride from hell is exactly what thirteen-year-old Kaitlyn received when she decided to go on the Tower of Power in June of 2007. On the afternoon of June 21st, Kaitlyn and two of her friends boarded the ride and took a trip to the top without incident. It was the first attraction they visited that day.

When the ride was over they noticed there wasn't a long line to ride again. They asked the operator if they could stay on for a second trip, which they did. As the girls started to make their second trip up, disaster struck. At about 25 feet up, the girls started to hear a clanging and whipping sound. Some of the metal cables for the ride broke and were falling down and landing on the girls. They were covered in the cables. Kaitlyn was covered the most as they were around her head, neck and legs.

Bleeding from being cut by the greasy metal wires the girls started screaming for the operator to stop the ride. The operator didn't stop it and the girls continued to the top. The ride finally leveled off and the girls were able to get most of the cables off of each other, except for one that was still wrapped around Kaitlyn's legs. As the ride plunged down, the cable shattered Kaitlyn's femur and severed both of her feet. She was rushed to the hospital where surgeons were able to reattach one foot.

Her two friends only received minor injuries, something Kailyn would have sustained had the ride been shut down as they screamed on their way up. When the state investigated they determined the cable failure was from fatigue. Despite being checked just one week prior, it was determined that if the park was operating from a newer ride manual they may have noticed the cable issues.

The cable failure and lack of response time to shut the ride down were the causes for Kaitlyn's injuries. Her family sued the park and before the case went to trial in November of 2008, Six Flags settled the suit without disclosing figures. The Superman Tower of Power was subsequently dismantled and removed from the park after Kaitlyn's accident.

Six Flags New England: Agawam, Massachusetts

Located just miles from the Connecticut-Massachusetts border is Six Flags New England. While the park has only been in the Six Flags family since 1998, the actual land the park sits on has been entertaining people since the late 1800s.

During the 1870s, New Englanders picnicked and relaxed on the grounds the park sits on. By the turn of the century the land was called Riverside Park and a few mechanical rides and a carousel debuted.

As the twentieth century progressed, Riverside Park became an amusement park. During the 1970s, the park received its first roller coaster, and by the year 2000, the park featured the east coast's tallest and longest roller coaster, Superman: Ride of Steel.

The Superman coaster (rethemed and renamed in 2009 as Bizarro) features a 221-foot drop and zooms along at speeds of 77 miles per hour on nearly one mile of track. In 2004, Superman was rated the number two coaster in the world according to *Amusement Today's* Golden Ticket Awards. It's not surprising then that fifty-five-year-old Stanley wanted to ride it when he went to the park that May.

Stanley was a special man and by special, I mean that in a good way. Despite being born with cerebral palsy and having a litany of health problems (lung, heart and diabetes issues later in life) he had a zest for life and made friends everywhere he went. Despite his disabilities and short yet robust stature--he was 5'2" and weighed around 230 lbs.--very little got in the way of Stanley getting what he wanted. After all, this was the guy who at twelve years old was pulled over by state police, after he took the local priest's car out for a joy ride.

One morning in May of 2004, when Stanley told his mother he was going to Six Flags New England by himself for the day, she wasn't surprised. These are the types of things he did. His independence and his happiness were his driving force. Tragically, everything would come to an end for Stanley that day due in part to a decision he and others made. Stanley was no stranger to Six Flags; he frequented the park often. He was also no stranger to the Superman coaster, as he rode it many times. Often, Stanley would ride his motor scooter right up the handicap entrance and board the ride like everyone else.

Other times he had to put up a fight to get on. In one instance after he was turned away, he went home and picked up his nephew. Stanley and his nephew then returned to the park and finagled a trip on the ride. Stanley told the ride operator his nephew was his "body guard."

As mentioned, this day would end differently for Stanley and his trip aboard Superman. Stanley got on the ride without a bodyguard or hassle from the ride operators. He boarded and was seated in the first row. Seconds later, the coaster was off.

Seated behind Stanley was a woman named Faith. When Faith was boarding the ride, she wondered to herself about Stanley's safety as a rider. Faith would wonder no more, when the ride left the platform and started up the first incline, as she saw Stanley coming out of his seat. She quickly sprung into action and started to hold on to him. As each hill approached she held on tighter and tighter, and Stanley slid further and further out of his seat.

At this point, Faith was not even holding on for her own safety. She was grasping on to anything she could to keep Stanley in his ride car. She clutched his shirt, suspenders and the belt around his waist, anything to keep him in his seat. As the ride made its way into its final hill and bank, Faith could hold on no longer. Stanley lost his grip as well. Tragically, he fell backwards out of the car, hit the track and then tumbled onto the pavement and fence below. Minutes later, an ambulance arrived and took Stanley to the hospital where he was pronounced dead.

Clearly the ride's restraint system didn't work for Stanley. The T-bar that was supposed to rest against his lap and safety belt used to secure him into his sear weren't fully locked. After the accident Faith even mentioned she witnessed the T-bar only being halfway down on Stanley's body. The Massachusetts

Department of Public Safety's accident report drew the same conclusions.

Stanley's size prevented the T-bar from being in the locked position. Had it been locked, he would have never left the car. The report also said the ride attendant failed to determine the adequacy of the restraint system in this situation. Had he done so, Stanley would have been denied entry to the ride. The investigation also partially faulted Stanley for going on the ride. As Stanley's mom was quoted by the Associated Press after the accident, "How could anybody as heavy as he was go up and spin up in the air like a yo-yo. It doesn't make any sense. He was over 200 pounds, maybe 225 pounds."

Since the accident, Six Flags has modified the ride's restraint system, revised its operations manual and retrained its staff. The company also settled a $1.5 million dollar lawsuit with Stanley's family in January of 2005.

Six Flags Great America: Gurnee, Illinois

Six Flags Great America is located just outside of Chicago, Illinois. The park opened in 1976 and became part of the Six Flags family in 1984. Over the years, the park has seen its fair share of accidents and incidents. The park's safety record became national news in 2007 when OSHA cited Six Flags Great America for 38 safety violations and fined them $117,000. OSHA's report outlined many violations, some repeat offenses, others new offenses. The violations at the park ran the gamut from failing to use approved pumps to dispense flammable liquids and improper storage to having sprinkler heads covered by plastic bags. The violations occurred during five OSHA park visits from 2004 to 2007.

OSHA's interest in Great America started back in 2004 when an employee was killed as he worked on a coaster. On May 28, 2004, the Illinois Department of Labor issued a permit to Six Flags allowing their new coaster, Ragin' Cajun, to open. The coaster is a steel "mouse" design found at amusement parks all over the world. This design is sometimes called a "wild" or "crazy" mouse, and they usually don't take up much real estate at the amusement park. The thrill ride features small cars that take very tight flat turns at a modest speed. Traditionally, there are no banks, loops or steep drops.

The day after the ride received its permit, a fifty-two-year-old employee named Jack was performing routine maintenance on the ride. As he was standing on the ground beneath the tracks, he was struck in the head by a passing car full of riders.

Two and a half weeks later, Jack succumbed to his head injuries. OSHA investigated and fined the park $8,867 and ordered the park to make safety changes. Jack's death wasn't the only workplace injury or death at the park. In August of 2007, a fifty-two-year-old worker was performing routine maintenance on a locomotive when he fell 20 feet off the train and landed on the ground. He was helicoptered to the hospital with spine injuries.

Another employee accident happened in March of 2008, when employee Thomas was working on dismantling the Splash Water Falls. Thomas fell more than 40 feet and died from his injuries. The accidents and incidents plaguing Six Flags Great America aren't exclusive to their work force. Over the years, many children have been involved in some nasty situations as well.

In June of 1997, a fourteen-year-old boy was injured while riding the park's Viper roller coaster. The Viper is a wooden roller coaster that debuted in 1995. It features an 80-foot drop and races to speeds close to 50 miles per hour. On that fateful day, as the young boy's coaster pulled back into the load area, investigators said the boy's arm was dangling outside of the ride as it approached. As the ride slowed to a stop, his arm became pinned between the ride car and platform. Firefighters had to use a miniature "jaws of life" to free his arm. Once free, he was airlifted to the hospital where tragically he lost a portion of his right hand.

Another story of a child losing part of an appendage also took place at Great America. Back in July of 2000, twelve-year-old Kati lost most of her right big toe in a ride accident aboard the Cajun Cliffhanger.

The Cliffhanger is a type of ride that is featured at amusement parks across the country. The attraction relies on one of the Newtonian laws of physics to keep riders thrilled and safe. Riders enter a circular room and stand against a wall. Slowly the room starts to rotate building up speed. As the speed builds, Centrifugal force keeps riders pinned against the wall, then the floor drops away.

As the ride comes to an end the spinning slows down and the riders make their way back down to the floor and exit the ride. Things didn't go as planned when Kati was riding the attraction with her father. After the ride initially slowed down, she started to slide down to the floor so she could exit the ride. Then suddenly, the ride sped up again and the floor was raised while the ride was still spinning. This is when Kati's foot got caught between the wall and the floor. Her foot was pinned and her toes were crushed.

It took a bit of time before workers could free her. Eventually, someone showed up with a crowbar and was able to get her free and transport her to the hospital. Kati's family sued the park and the case went to court. During the lawsuit, Kati's attorney's obtained documents that showed the ride had complaints from 13 other riders since 1993, a half dozen of which resulted in injuries. In March of 2002, Kati settled with the park for an undisclosed sum. What was disclosed from the settlement was the provision that called for Six Flags to either take down the ride at its parks nationwide or install a rubber safety strip to help prevent similar accidents. The attraction at Great America was removed from the park. Oh yeah, the little rubber safety strip that would have prevented an accident like this would have cost roughly $5.

In May of 2003, eleven-year-old Erica boarded the Raging Bull roller coaster. The ride is a steel-built hyper twister. It features steep banks, speeds over 70 miles an hour, and a 200-foot drop on almost one mile of track. Moments after riding the nearly 3-minute coaster, Erica collapsed. Paramedics at the park were summoned and they worked to revive her; they were unsuccessful.

When Erica's story first broke, the preliminary hypothesis was she choked on a piece of gum or taffy while she was on the ride. Six Flags was already equipped with signs warning folks not to eat, drink or chew gum while riding. After Erica's incident, they posted additional signs. Months later, in December, a formal autopsy was released and it indicated Erica was chewing gum while she was on the attraction, but that wasn't her cause of death. The coroner determined she had a pre-existing medical condition that caused her death, an enlarged heart.

In August of 2006, a similar situation played out for a ten-year-old girl who passed away after she collapsed at the park. In this situation, the young girl and her family were well aware of her history with heart trouble. The little girl had just gotten off a ride at the Camp Cartoon area of the park. As she was running to join her family, she collapsed and was pronounced dead at the hospital.

Sadly, it isn't just coasters or thrill rides that can cause heart trouble for park-goers. As history reveals, some of the attractions at water parks are also taxing for those with pre-existing conditions.

This was the case at Great America in June 2005 when lifeguards sprang into action to help save a man after he collapsed from his stint at the park's wave pool. The sixty-eight-year-old man passed away at the hospital from a heart attack.

The addition of water parks has become a popular business addition for many amusement parks across the country. Six Flags has capitalized on this industry trend as well. Unfortunately, a quick survey of the incidents at many of these parks shows these locations can become a hotbed for perverts and pedophiles.

One such incident happened in June of 2010 when an off-duty police officer was visiting Great America's Hurricane Harbor water park for the day. When the man went into the men's locker room to use the facilities, he noticed someone holding a cell phone under his stall and recording video.

The officer confronted the man who took off on foot. After a brief chase, the officer got his man, and he was turned over to the Gurnee police. Police arrested thirty-nine-year-old Chicago elementary school teacher, Jamie. When they searched his phone, they found images of men and boys in various stages of undress. Jamie was charged with one count of unauthorized video recording and live video transmission. In September of 2010, Jamie pled guilty to the charge and was sentenced to two years probation.

A similar situation happened in August 2012, when a nineteen-year-old park employee was arrested for peeping on 2 twelve-year-old girls as they changed in a dressing room at Hurricane Harbor. Twenty-year-old Jamie was sentenced to two years probation after pleading guilty to misdemeanor invasion of privacy charges. A difference in this case was that it took place at Six Flags St. Louis, which is our next destination.

Six Flags St. Louis, Eureka, Missouri

The opening year for Six Flags Over Mid-America was 1971. The park is located in a suburb of St. Louis and is known today as Six Flags St. Louis. Long before the park changed names in

Amusement Park 9-1-1

1996, it was the scene for two deadly accidents.

In July of 1978, a gondola ride that carried visitors some 70 to 100 feet across the width of the park failed. Around 2:00 in the afternoon on a hot and humid day, one of the support arms on a tower broke, and a gondola slipped off of its cable. The gondola went crashing to the ground killing three of its four occupants. A ten-year-old, a fifteen-year-old and their twenty-five-year old uncle passed away. The fourth passenger was critically injured but survived the 7-story fall. Thankfully, only 15 of 28 gondolas were operating at the time, and the safety mechanisms kicked in on all the other cars so they didn't come crashing down.

The park deemed the situation a "freak accident" and noted over 15 million people rode the gondolas without incident. After an inspection, engineers determined the support arm failed after a cracked and rusty bolt snapped. In November of 1978, the families of the three visitors that died and the fourth victim, who was left with permanent injuries, sued both Six Flags and the Swiss manufacturer of the gondola. The cases were eventually settled out of court.

The last tragedy at Six Flags Mid-America happened in July of 1984. The River King Mine Train was the park's first roller coaster and debuted when the park opened in 1971. The coaster is a hybrid wooden coaster and is still in operation today. For a brief stint in 1984 the coaster was modified and received a name change. The ride became known as the Rail Blazer and was refitted into a stand-up coaster.

Less than a month after the park made the changes to the coaster forty-six-year-old Stella was fatally ejected from the ride as she rode along with her husband. After the accident, Stella's husband scoffed at the notion that she was too heavy to ride the attraction or that she passed out before she was flung from the ride.

He mentioned the two were holding hands when the ride made a sharp "whipping" motion and she was thrown over fifty feet. Stella was pronounced dead at a local hospital due to blunt trauma to the head and chest. The usual series of events unfolded in the wake of Stella's death. There was an investigation, a lawsuit and then a change. In this case, a mechanical engineer hired by St. Louis County led the investigation. The investigation centered on the restraint system of the ride, which consisted of a shoulder harness and knee brace bound together by a buckled strap.

The engineer determined the restraint system could cause "personal discomfort" to "a very few extremely large body types" when securely fastened (Stella was 5 feet 7 inches tall and weighed more than 200 pounds). He declared it doubtful that the ride loaders would close the restraint to such an extreme position to cause discomfort in every case. With that being said, persons of a certain girth could make their way out of the safety harness, if it wasn't fastened tight enough. No single factor caused the mishap but a number of factors probably contributed, including Stella not holding onto the safety bar with both hands, as she was holding her husband's hand. In the weeks after the investigation Stella's husband filed a lawsuit against the park, which was later settled, and Six Flags changed the ride back to its original form and name.

As we make our way across the Midwest, we have one more stop in Colorado before we end up in at our final destination, California, and the slew of accidents and incidents that plagued the Six Flags parks on the west coast.

Six Flags Elitch Gardens: Denver, Colorado (1999-2006)

Elitch Gardens, as it is known today, is a seasonally operated amusement park that Six Flags no longer owns. For a few years in the early part of the new millennium, this park was under the umbrella of Six Flags. Under their ownership the company made several prominent additions to the park, most notably in the way of coasters, the Boomerang, Half-Pipe and the Flying Coaster. The additions of these coasters certainly created buzz for coaster enthusiasts, but it was two other existing coasters that stole the headlines on the national news scene.

Remember in the beginning of the chapter the blurb about Six Flags conducting research into amusement park rides and brain injuries, they determined there was no safety risk, and all was safe. Well, Deborah will probably tell you otherwise after her trip to Six Flags Elitch Gardens in 1997. Deborah's story was featured in a June 2002, New York Times article about thrill rides and brain trauma.

It seems Deborah was having just another day at an amusement park like millions of us do each year. Her sons coaxed her onto the park's coaster, the Mind Eraser, a suspended coaster with a series of loops, inversions and high speeds. From the first drop on the coaster Deborah knew she was in trouble. Her harness was loose and her head bobbed and weaved accordingly, mimicking the coasters every move.

"At the bottom of the hill my head was forced back and hit the back of the seat," she said. "On the loops, my head knocked against the sides of the headrest. I passed out briefly. When the ride halted, I was dazed. I had to steady myself against a pole in order to stand."

In the days following the ride, she felt a myriad of symptoms, memory loss, nausea, dizziness, blurred vision, and periodic blackouts. She even awoke one morning to a bloody left eye. These symptoms led her to see a neurologist, who diagnosed her with a traumatic brain injury, short-term memory loss, vertigo and ocular damage.

This diagnosis came roughly two months after riding the coaster. Deborah filed an accident report with the park and later sued them. Not shockingly, the suit was settled confidentially out of court. Thankfully, Deborah did live to tell her tale, and she does suffer permanent deficits from her trip to the amusement park. Deborah's situation isn't an everyday occurrence at an amusement park but as these stories recount, they happen more often than one would expect.

Now obviously folks aren't going to stop and see their local neurologist and ask for an MRI of their brains before they go to an amusement park. If you or a loved one have an underlying condition, such as elevated blood pressure (of which, an effect of this could be a stroke or heart attack), again, heed the warnings posted out in front of each and every ride and don't take the chance or be a hero.

With that public service announcement out of the way, it's now time to visit the Six Flags parks in the state of California. It is the last component of the Six Flags chapter and is filled with some interesting stories both heart wrenching and head scratching.

Six Flags in California: Magic Mountain and Discovery Kingdom

In the shadow of the legendary Disneyland is Six Flag's most popular (Six Flags Great Adventure in New Jersey is number two in the company) amusement park, Magic Mountain in Valencia, California. The amusement park is located roughly 40 miles northwest of Los Angeles and has a yearly attendance of 2.9 million people. Since the park opened in 1971 it has been at the forefront of the roller coaster revolution in America.

Today, Magic Mountain holds the record for the most roller coasters at an amusement park. With the large variety of coasters and rides to choose from, the park has become no stranger to accidents over the years. However, ride accidents haven't been the only subject to make headlines. With Southern California's propensity for street gangs, some gang related violence also seeped into the park.

Amusement Park 9-1-1

Picking up right where we left off with brain injuries, in June of 2001, twenty-eight-year-old Pearl boarded the Goliath roller coaster. Goliath certainly lives up to its name, as it takes riders on a 3-minute, 85-mile-per-hour journey of spirals, twists and drops at heights nearing 255 feet. When Goliath opened in February of 2000, it quickly became one of the most popular attractions at the park.

Roughly a year and a half after the rides debut, Pearl boarded the coaster for her 3-minute journey. As we've seen all too often, when Pearl's ride car pulled back into the load area, she was slumped over and unconscious. She was rushed to the hospital where she was pronounced dead. The OSHA investigation of the ride revealed everything was operating correctly.

The autopsy performed on Pearl by the Los Angeles County Coroners office determined Pearl had a pre-existing aneurysm that ruptured (which she did not know about) along with hemorrhaging around her brain stem. The coroner determined "the stress associated with the roller coaster probably was a factor in her death."

Despite the overwhelming success of the ride, a very small percentage of riders (numbering in the teens) have reportedly "blacked out" while they were aboard. Today, the Goliath is still going strong with millions of riders enjoying the ride.

Do you recall the gondola accident back in 1978 at Six Flags in St. Louis? Well, a few months before that accident, a similar one happened the same year at Magic Mountain. In February, twenty-three-year old Miguel and his new bride, twenty-four-year old Cathy had just finished up their wedding ceremony and drove 25 miles to Magic Mountain to begin their honeymoon. The newlyweds boarded the Eagles Flight Sky ride for a panoramic view of the park. Just 100 feet from the load area, Miguel and Cathy's gondola started to sway back and forth. Their gondola slipped off its supporting cable and went crashing down to the ground from 50 feet above. The newlyweds were rushed to the hospital in critical condition. Miguel passed away hours later at the hospital, while Cathy was able to pull through.

The next two accidents at Magic Mountain involved park employees. Back in May of 1996, at Revolution, the world's first modern coaster with a vertical loop, claimed the life of a part-time employee. Twenty-five-year-old Cherie apparently violated one of the park's safety rules: never set foot on the tracks in front of a coaster. Cherie made this fateful move when she was switching positions with another employee at 3:00 P.M. Cherie was set to shift from the passenger-unloading platform to the passenger-loading platform. This shift is something the company has employees do to keep them alert and prevent boredom. The industry claims the shift has improved ride safety.

Unfortunately, Cherie's effort for better safety ended up causing her demise. Cherie was trying to scurry across the tracks when the six-ton coaster pulled back into the station at roughly four miles per hour and struck her. This hit forced her to fall into the shallow pit beneath the tracks where she sustained many fatal injuries. Cherie's death was the first employee death in the park's history.

Regrettably, when Cherie's accident happened, the park was open and there were several park-goers and employees that witnessed the accident. Eight years later a similar accident happened when a coaster fatally struck another employee.

At the time, twenty-one-year-old Bantita, a Thai law student working at the park as part of a summer work program, was gearing up for her shift at the coaster Scream! The ride is a floorless coaster that features seven inversions and reaches speeds of over 60 miles an hour.

For reasons unknown, Bantita was underneath the track of

the ride when she was struck and killed by one of the ride cars as it went through its pre-opening morning paces. California OSHA determined the accident was purely accidental, and they didn't know why she deviated from her safety training and walked underneath the attraction to a restricted area.

The final collection of stories from Magic Mountain doesn't deal with accidents but violence and some erratic behavior. Back in June of 1985, Magic Mountain was hosting an all night "School's Out" party for some Los Angeles area high schools. That evening some 25,000 kids descended upon the park. Some of the kids in attendance were members of rival gangs from the San Fernando Valley.

As the evening wore on, tensions rose and the two gangs decided to rumble at the park. Despite an increased police presence (the park heard rumors there may be some gang violence and arranged for an additional eleven deputies on site), around 2:15 A.M., near a dance pavilion, a fight broke out between the two groups.

In the rumble, four park security guards were assaulted and six young men were stabbed. Each of the stabbing victims was transported to the hospital with wounds to the arms, chest or buttocks. The deputy's on site were having trouble corralling the gang members and called in for reinforcements. Once 25 more officers arrived, they were able to make peace and arrest 21 people on charges ranging from felony assault with a deadly weapon to misdemeanor trespassing.

As Scott Piazza, park spokesman, said at the time, "I don't think it was related to the all-night party. The party just happened to be going that night, and they were in the mood to do something." Scott was probably spot-on with that comment.

During the 1980s, and even today the park is very cognizant of the gang climate in their area. In the past the security force of the park collaborated with the Los Angeles County Sheriff's

Department and their Operation Safe Streets Gang Unit to keep the park safe. The units patrolled the parking lots, confiscated any contraband and circulated through the park to keep the gang violence at a minimum.

In 1993, these security patrols were tested when a melee in the park swelled to several hundred kids. The kids left Magic Mountain and wreaked havoc at a local Wendy's and gas station, assaulting and vandalizing anyone or anything they encountered.

In 1998 there was a gang related shooting that claimed the life of a fifteen-year-old boy at a parking lot adjacent to the park. Since these incidents, by and large park security did a good job maintaining order, sometimes too good of a job if you ask some park visitors.

After the stabbing in 1985, Magic Mountain adopted a new screening policy to keep gang members out. When the policy was implemented, critics called it overly aggressive. The policy allegedly allowed park employees to stop and interrogate any person they thought was a possible gang member. Stopping them was based solely on appearance. If the park employee didn't like the responses from the person they were questioning, they were allegedly asked to leave. Sometimes the questioning and subsequent exit from the park were even videotaped. Under this screening policy many folks claimed they were discriminated against because they were African American or Latino. They claimed they were stopped, questioned and then escorted out for no reason.

The situation came to a head in 1989, when Six Flags settled two lawsuits filed by the American Civil Liberties Union on behalf of two families who claimed they were accused of being gang members by park security based exclusively on being Latino and the clothing they wore.

As the years went by, the complaints continued to roll in.

Most complaints alleged racial discrimination. By 2001, the situation came to another climax when four lawsuits (one of them had 30 plaintiffs) were filed against the park in Los Angeles Superior Court. The suits accused the park of improper racial profiling, harassment, assault and unlawful detainment. The four cases were eventually certified for class action status, and over 150 people became involved. The members of the lawsuit were an interesting mix of people. There was Israel, a 1984 Olympic bronze medal winning boxer from Sierra Leone, members of church groups, school children and a group of librarians. In 2004, Six Flags agreed to settle the lawsuit for $5.6 million. When the settlement was announced the park denied any wrongdoing and said they merely wanted to settle to put the situation behind them.

"We've never discriminated against anybody," said Sue Carpenter, a spokeswoman for Six Flags California. "In the past, Magic Mountain has employed a security-screening program that it believed was lawful and protective. We continue to enforce our strict rules for appropriate conduct for all visitors and employees of the park. "

Before the class action suit came together, the park had a few other alleged racial incidents that brought them into court. In January of 1988 an African-American family sued Magic Mountain after a worker at the game "Set em up" allegedly hurled the N word at them after a dispute at the carnival game. The park offered a settlement of $35,000.

Another alleged racial situation was between an African-American park-goer and an employee in 1999. The man claimed some racial epitaphs were used to describe him when he went on the bungee jump ride, Dive Devil. After the man took his plunge he decided to buy the videotape featuring his jump. When he got home and viewed the recording, he heard racist and disparaging comments made about him in the background. The park claimed there was no way to determine if the comments were made by the employees or other park-goers, as there were hundreds of people around the attraction.

The last case before we head up the coast to Six Flag's Discovery Kingdom was handled by an attorney who is still working the legal and media scene. Over twenty-five years later, none other than Gloria Allred was the representing lawyer in the case.

It seems back in May 1985, Valerie called Magic Mountain and asked to reserve the park for a special "gay pride" event. The park turned her down and said they encountered too many problems back in 1979 when the park hosted a gay night.

Back in 1979, several teenage employees failed to report to work that night. In addition, the park received 75 complaints from parents of staff members who were critical of the event. So based off of prior experience they couldn't honor Valerie's request. In fact, in court documents (as mentioned with Gloria Allred, Valerie sued), the park claimed that teenagers made up an even greater proportion of the work force in 1984 than back in 1979.

About 75% of its 2,000 employees were teenagers and while the park has no policy against admitting homosexuals, Magic Mountain officials feared that they would encounter "impossible staffing problems with an event reserved exclusively for homosexuals," former general manager Richard Miller told the court in a written declaration. As the parks spokesman stated at the time, "with increasing concern about the high incidence of acquired immune deficiency syndrome in the gay community, many employees do not want to be in a concentrated setting of high-risk individuals."

Wow, a crazy statement there looking back now. In July of 1986, the court ruled that Magic Mountain illegally discriminated against homosexuals. The court rejected the argument that teenagers might refuse to show up for work due to a fear of AIDS.

Amusement Park 9-1-1

Six Flags Discovery Kingdom: Vallejo, California

The stories from Discovery Kingdom may give you flashbacks to the SeaWorld chapter. The two parks are very similar in their theme, shows and unfortunately animal/marine life attacks. Discovery Kingdom was originally known as Marine World when it opened in 1968. Thirty years later, in 1998, Marine World joined the Six Flags brand, which solidified the parks' expansion into the thrill ride arena.

With the addition of rides came the inevitable accident or two. In August of 1999, a faulty cable on the coaster, Boomerang, stranded 28 riders in midair for several hours. A month later, a nine-year-old boy slipped out of his safety restraint and fell from the Scat-a-bout ride. In 2001 and 2002, a forty-one year old and nine year old were injured when they rode the Starfish.

Like SeaWorld, most of the tragic stories or controversy from this park are centered around the critters they have on display. The debate and controversy that festers with Sea World, to an extent also plagues Discovery Kingdom. The park previously featured a killer whale named Shouka, who was dubbed the "worlds loneliest whale," as she lived a life in solitude at Discovery Kingdom. Killer whales and dolphins are highly social and need companionship. For a period, Discovery Kingdom had Shouka living with a bottlenose dolphin, but eventually issues arose between the two of them and they had to go their separate ways.

Aside from the issues of sharing her tank with a dolphin, Shouka wasn't always happy living at Discovery Kingdom. At times, she certainly let her displeasure be known. In acts of frustration, Shouka gnawed on the steel link fence resulting in damage to her mouth and breaking nearly all of her teeth.

Additional acts of aggression were shared with the world when video surfaced on YouTube that captured Shouka becoming aggressive with her trainer during a show. By the end of 2012, Six Flags sent Shouka to SeaWorld in San Diego, so she could finally have companionship with other killer whales. Shouka's disgruntled behavior wasn't the only flash of aggression between animal and human. The trainers at Discovery Kingdom had brushes with elephants, tigers and cougars—the cats, not older ladies prowling for younger men!

In all seriousness, back in January of 1996, two trainers at then Marine World, were attacked by two cougars at the park's Africa USA area. Trainer Greg, and his back-up Chad went in to take one of the cougars for a walk. At the time, cougars Zuni and Tonto were playing together in their enclosure. Greg entered their area and the cats began to play with him as well. Initially, the playing was tame. Soon it escalated to aggressive behavior and the cats began to bite and scratch at Greg.

The other trainer, Chad, was serving as Greg's back-up and entered the enclosure to pull him out. Both men were rushed to the hospital, with Greg being admitted to the intensive care unit for a few severe bites. Thankfully, Chad only sustained minor injuries. This was the first publicized incident of aggressive behavior from the cougars; luckily both men lived to tell about it.

Two years later in August of 1998, Chad found himself in another dangerous situation with an attacking cat. This time the situation wasn't with trainers looking to exercise or play with animals. The situation happened when a 340-pound Bengal tiger named Kuma got spooked and mauled a woman who was posing with the cat for a picture.

Back in the day, for $250, visitors could go backstage at Marine World and have their photo taken with Kuma; it was a part of the park's "Phenomenal Photo Program." By all accounts Kuma was a well-behaved animal. He sat for over 100 pictures with members of the public. In 1998, Jaunell was one of those visitors who wanted a picture with the tiger. Before she made her way backstage, Jaunell was given a set of rules to follow.

Amusement Park 9-1-1

One of the rules was if Kuma stands up, you stand up. When Jaunell approached the photo session, Kuma was lying down. Jaunell was instructed to kneel down on a two-foot high platform next to the cat, which she did. Suddenly, Kuma stood up and Jaunell followed, or tried to follow. As she made her move to stand, she lost her balance and fell off her platform. Jaunell's fall scared the tiger and he lunged on top of her, jaw wide open. As Jaunell recounted about her fall years later:

"And the tiger said, 'Oh, there's a toy.' But it's a cat, and when they play, they play to kill. I closed down my chin to protect my neck, and that's why he got my face. He bit through my head, damaged my vertebra and my ear canal. The bottom third of my face was on my chest. They had to sew all of that back."

With Kuma believing Jaunell was a play toy, Chad and other trainers sprang into action to free her. The trainers were shouting commands and trying to free Jaunell, to no avail. Finally, a trainer came in and sprayed a fire extinguisher, which scared Kuma enough for him to stop and release her. Jaunell was rushed to the hospital, and underwent several surgeries. She eventually made a full recovery.

The last animal versus human incident happened in June of 2004. This story is actually a sad one on many levels. That day in June, trainer Patrick was standing next to twenty-three-year-old African elephant, Misha, while she grazed in a grassy field. Misha suddenly turned towards Patrick, knocked him over and gored him in front of a handful of park visitors. Another trainer saw the act and shouted towards Misha to get her away from Patrick, which she did. Paramedics moved in and Patrick was airlifted to the hospital in critical condition with deep wounds to his abdomen.

After a successful surgery Patrick made a full recovery. The same couldn't be said for Misha. After the unprovoked attack, she was isolated from the other elephants housed at Discovery

Kingdom. That was until she was packed into a crate and trucked 700 miles to Utah's Hogle Zoo in April 2005.

Misha's stint at the zoo lasted until September 2008, when at the age of twenty-seven, she was put to sleep (elephants in the wild can live up to 60 years). As Patrick commented upon learning of Misha's death, he felt the elephant gave up the will to live. Misha stopped eating and was down to 6,000 pounds from a one-time 7,400 pounds. She had trouble standing and was listless. The tough decision was made to put her down. Misha's life wasn't an easy one. She was born in Africa and removed from her family at two years old and ended up in what we know today as Discovery Kingdom.

Over the years, much larger and aggressive elephants picked on Misha; often she was a victim of their physical attacks. One such attack led to an open wound near her mouth. The wound became infected and required treatments from the park's vets. During one treatment session, the vets broke a surgical instrument in her jaw, and they were never able to retrieve it. If that wasn't stressful enough for her, one year the park tried to impregnate her. This resulted in a stillborn baby and a lasting infection in the incision they created for the procedure.

It was a tough go at things for both Misha and Discovery Kingdom. At one point, the California based non-profit, *In Defense of Animals* placed the park on its list of "10 Worst Zoos for Elephants" noting that nine elephants had died at the amusement park since 1995, a death rate they calculated at the time of one every sixteen months, noting that most of the elephants weren't elderly but middle-aged. Sadly, we know what became of Misha. Luckily, the fate and reputation of Discovery Kingdom fared better than the troubled pachyderm. Their accidents and incidents have been at a minimum.

The park still showcases animals and animal encounters, quite successfully, with the exception of one recent encounter when something went awry. This time the animal wasn't the aggressor, but a jackass was (a foolish person, not a donkey!). The odd story happened back in May 2008, when a twenty-four-year-old man scaled an animal enclosure and smacked a camel on its hindquarters. The Arabian camel (dromedary) named Dakar was a little shocked and spooked by the antics, but was otherwise okay.

A sixteen-year-old witness saw the man's actions and reported it to an educational guide, who then alerted security and called police. When police arrived they were originally only going to cite the man for the incident. After questioning him, he panicked and fled on foot. He jumped into a waiting car and sped off. After a brief highway chase police (all over smacking a camel, mind you) arrested the camel slapper and his get-a-way car driver. The slapper was arrested on suspicion of misdemeanor cruelty to animals and a misdemeanor probation violation—which he said might be for a DUI or maybe a petty theft. After he posted bail, the smacker figured he would cash in on his newfound "fame." He listed the sneakers he was wearing when he slapped the camel on eBay and named the auction, "camel slapper shoes." Judging by the statement released by Six Flags at the time, the park and animal lovers from all around had much to say about the incident:

"That's really obnoxious, and it's so disrespectful," park spokeswoman Nancy Chan said Thursday. "He should actually be apologizing for his actions rather than doing something like that, which is not funny." Chan said some park visitors have submitted online comments calling him a "despicable human being" and urging the park to pursue charges.

This closes out the chapter on Six Flags and the unfortunate accidents that happen from time to time. Rider error, operator error and unknown pre-existing health conditions, often seem to be the catalyst for tragedy. Errors and health conditions aside, it seems there has even been situations at Six Flags where coasters had design flaws that weren't fully realized until after a rider was injured during their trip. This was the situation on both the Texas Cyclone at Houston's AstroWorld and the Georgia Cyclone at Six Flags over Georgia.

At AstroWorld, Six Flags added headrests to the coaster after the jarring movements of the ride left a sixteen-year-old with a ruptured vein in his neck, which in turn sent a blood clot to his brain. The clot then left him partially paralyzed. A similar situation happened down in Georgia when a thirty-one-year-old rider heard her neck crack and then felt her right arm go numb. It was revealed that she broke her neck after the ride's first hill. Six Flags re-engineered the ride and took out some of the hills and loops.

Through it all though, ride safety and park safety is every amusement company's "bread and butter." Their whole business plan and reputation is based upon it.

Understandably, safety is something that directly affects the fiscal bottom line. Accidents or bad publicity tarnishes their reputation, whether the park is negligent or not. The after-shocks of accidents have been reflected in both individual ride and park attendance.

This has been acknowledged by Six Flags in their filings with the Securities and Exchange Commission (SEC). In a document titled Form 8-K (it announces things to shareholders, like corporate risk, etc.) Six Flags states:

"Almost all of our parks feature "thrill rides." While we carefully maintain the safety of our rides, there are inherent risks involved with these attractions. An accident or an injury at any of our parks or at parks operated by our competitors may reduce attendance at our parks, causing a decrease in revenues."

Despite the claims and insistence not only by Six Flags but the amusement park industry in general that this industry is one of the safest things to do in the world, strokes, death or heart attacks still loom over the industry.

These events become national news stories that garner a lot of attention, which is something every amusement park is cognizant of. Any accident is tragic and unfortunate and statistics don't lie. Just remember your odds of being put to death by legal execution are 1 in 96,203!

BUSCH GARDENS

In 2013, Busch Gardens held two positions on the top twenty most visited amusement parks in North America. Their location in Tampa, Florida was number 12 and Williamsburg, Virginia was number 20. As their name alludes to, the parks were owned and operated by the Anheuser-Busch Company. This mainstay in American brewing used these parks as a way to promote and market their products to the country.

During the beer maker's foray into amusement park ownership, they had as many as four parks operating across the country. The parks featured onsite breweries and gave samples of free suds to the masses. As time went on, two of the four parks ceased operations~ California and Texas— as did the free beer samples.

The two remaining amusement parks have changed hands over the years and are now owned and operated by the same group that operates SeaWorld. The park in Williamsburg, Virginia is where our stories will start. The park debuted in 1975 with a European theme.

The passing decades have seen a few name changes to the park, Busch Gardens Europe to Busch Gardens Old Country. In between and back again, it was Busch Gardens, Williamsburg. The park features several European-themed villages and hamlets. Dispersed through these areas are a bevy of roller coasters and thrill rides, which bring us right back to coaster accidents. This time instead of starting the chapter with doom and gloom let's open up with an accident that is more noteworthy and less tragic, unless you're a goose.

In March of 1999, book cover model (my budget for this

book was really small; as you can see from the cover, I couldn't afford him!) and one-time faux butter spokes hunk Fabio went to Busch Gardens in Williamsburg to promote the park's new thrill ride, Apollo's Chariot. The ride is a steel coaster that reaches speeds of over 70 miles an hour, and features a 210-foot drop.

On the ride's maiden voyage, Fabio sat in the first row of the ride car. His job was very simple - do exactly what made him famous. Sit there and smile for the cameras. Two minutes later, when the ride was over and his car pulled back in, it appeared as though there was some sort of accident. Fabio wasn't all smiles like the park promoters expected. Instead, he was covered in blood. During his ride, there was a collision; Fabio's face met a goose head on. Other than a bloody nose, everything was A-okay for the big man. As for the bird, it was never seen again!

The final story from Busch Gardens, Williamsburg is no laughing matter. The crime itself didn't take place at the amusement park, but at the neighboring water park, Water Country USA. In August of 2008, four females visiting the park claimed a park employee sexually assaulted them. Two women and 2 eleven-year-old girls were on the park's Malibu Pipeline flume ride, when a park employee grabbed their breasts and in one case touched between one of the young girl's thighs. The women and children notified the park, and the man was taken into custody. Twenty-two-year-old Sandeep was in the country from India on a work visa. After the incident, he was arrested and charged with two felony aggravated battery sexual battery counts on children under thirteen and two misdemeanor sexual battery counts.

In 2009, Sandeep was convicted of the charges and spent fifteen months in jail until he was deported back to India. During his trial, Sandeep was asked why he did these horrible things. He claimed the touching was a misunderstanding on his part. It was a cultural thing; he claimed he had no idea that one doesn't grope children or women in their breast or genital areas in America.

He didn't think what he did was inappropriate, and was unaware of American customs. While justice was served in the criminal case, it wasn't in the civil case. In 2011, the group of women sued the park for $5.3 million; a jury determined the park was not liable. Leaving one crazy story for a few others. These next tales take place down at Busch Gardens in Tampa, Florida.

Over the past few years the price of precious and scrap metal has skyrocketed. It seems as though companies have popped up overnight looking to purchase any scrap or unwanted metal you can find. Unfortunately, this has led to some less than honorable people doing just that. Grabbing any metal they can find, scrapping it and getting a quick payday.

The news is filled with all kinds of creative and idiotic stories of unscrupulous people stealing what isn't theirs. The thefts range from the metal adornments from gravestones to the brass brake pads for a roller coaster—yep, you heard that right.

Back in August of 2011, a Busch Gardens roller coaster mechanic was arrested at a metal recycling business for trying to scrap 97 pounds of brass plates. Little did Richard know, but the Hillsborough County Sheriff's office stepped up their metal theft investigative unit. Richard learned about this investigative unit when he entered a metal scrap business and tried to cash in. Detectives just happened to be onsite and watched him turn in several brass plates for cash.

After the transaction, which was worth around $1,100, detectives moved in and asked him where the metal came from. Richard informed them he worked at Busch Gardens and took the scrap metal from his job. Authorities investigated and learned the brass plates were actually roller coaster brake pads. Richard took them without the park's permission. He was subsequently arrested.

Since the park in Tampa debuted in 1959, there have been a few name changes. Busch Gardens Africa, Busch Gardens: The Dark Continent and today, it's just Busch Gardens, Tampa. The names may have changed over the years and thrill rides may have seeped in, but the park is still animal-centric and is accredited by the Association of Zoos and Aquariums. Today, the park features numerous animal attractions and up close and personal experiences. For one park-goer, the experience was a bit too close for her liking.

This next story could probably make Dakar, the camel from Discovery Kingdom, mentioned in the last chapter, a little satisfied. Perhaps it was a small bit of animal retribution. In 2005, Busch Gardens was sued over a "vicious" peacock attack—true story here. This human and peacock encounter certainly became one for the books, the legal books that is.

In 2000, Elnita was wandering around the park, enjoying the day with her family. During her visit, she came across another two-legged creature that also cruises around the park, a peacock. Allegedly, as their two paths crossed, Elnita claimed the bird attacked her. The bird pecked at her hand, which startled her and caused her to fall flat on her back.

Elnita now claims she suffers from permanent nerve damage to her hand and back pain from her fall. This ferocious attack has kept her from holding a steady job. She was unable to resume her occupation as a hair braider, and filed sued against the park seeking at least $1 million to cover future loss of income. The case was eventually settled out of court.

Unusual animal lawsuit aside, the park has been plagued with some very serious and tragic accidents over the years. In February of 1989, elephant trainer Joseph was helping to feed Casey, a 3-ton male elephant. Suddenly, the elephant either knocked Joseph to the ground or he tripped and fell. Casey then proceeded to use his massive head to crush him. Joseph later died at the hospital from his injuries. Months later, OSHA investigated and cited the park for serious safety violations. They ordered new safety procedures to be implemented so the situation doesn't repeat itself. As for Casey, he was removed from the park and ended up at a breeding center.

The last notable animal incident happened in May of 2002, when a young zookeeper had her arm torn off by a 360-pound lion named Max. On that fateful day, twenty-one-year-old Amanda arranged for her family to have a private tour of the lion quarters. For more than a year, Amanda worked around the lions, and was training to draw blood when needed. Having witnessed and assisted in the procedure numerous times, she arranged to perform a simulated blood draw from Max while her family watched.

A blood draw, or in this case, a simulated one is a multi-step process. Over several years and through positive reinforcement and conditioning, Max was trained to lie down in a cage so blood could be drawn from his tail—he had a liver disorder that requires periodic blood tests. Rather than continuing to put him under anesthesia, vets and trainers devised this conditioning program. With Max calm in his cage, trainers draw the blood while another trainer sits by his head and hand feeds him meat. As mentioned, Amanda assisted in the mock blood draw in front of her family.

Everything went as planned until the end. With the procedure over, Amanda casually stood up and looped one of her fingers around the bar of Max's cage. In the blink of an eye, Max lunged and clamped down on Amanda's finger. A struggle between them ensued, a struggle we know Amanda will lose. Tragically, the situation came to an end when Max severed Amanda's arm at the elbow. Amanda and her limb were rushed to the hospital, but surgeons were unable to reattach it.

Kermit Gonzalo

What would a chapter about amusement park accidents be without another aerial gondola accident? Busch Gardens, Tampa was the scene for one in July 2009. This time, the outcome was much better than the previously mentioned ones.

At the time, twenty-year-old Maikon was working the Skyway ride at the park. After sending three passengers out in their gondola, he thought their door might be unlocked. He rushed towards the gondola and grabbed on to check it. Unfortunately, he held on too long and the car left the platform. The gondola was now on its trip across the park. As the gondola passed over a landscaped area at a height of 35 feet, Maikon finally let go and dropped to the ground. He landed on his feet and was taken to the hospital.

MRIs and scans revealed he had a compression fracture to his thoracic vertebrae—something that could be detrimental to everyone, let alone someone who was the starting placekicker for the University of South Florida's football team. Thankfully, Maikon made a full recovery and as of 2014 was trying to latch on to an NFL team as their starting kicker.

Do you recall the lightning strike story at SeaWorld in Chapter Two? The bolt touched down in the park and luckily there were no serious injuries. Unfortunately, seventy miles to the west in Tampa, at Busch Garden's Adventure Islands water park, a similar event happened but with a more tragic outcome.

In September 2011, a severe thunderstorm rolled into the area. As the storm loomed over the park, Justin, who just turned twenty-one the previous day, was working as a lifeguard supervisor at the six stories high, Key West Rapids water slide. As Justin watched over the attraction, he was standing in two-to-three feet of water— which is very dangerous when lightning is in the air.

Tragically, Justin was fatally struck by lightning (the odds of being struck by lightning in the U.S. are 1 in 700,000). With Justin hit, his co-workers pulled him from a shallow section of the slide and tried to resuscitate him, to no avail. What some consider a freak accident of Mother Nature, many consider a preventable death. Justin's parents sued the park in 2013 blaming them for his death.

Since the park opened in 1980, it's been equipped with real time weather tracking and monitoring for lightning strikes and incoming storm fronts. According to court filings, when the system detects lightning within 5 miles of the park, the park is supposed to shut down the rides. Allegedly on that day, the park didn't follow their standing protocol fast enough and didn't evacuate the water attractions with lightning present in the area. Quoting directly from the lawsuit:

"Between 10:14 and 11:34 A.M. that day, the equipment detected nine separate instances of lightning strikes within zero to five miles of the park. At 11:44 A.M., there were seven simultaneous lightning strikes at respective distances of two, seven, 1.2, 1.8, 2.6, three and 3.8 miles from the entrances of Adventure Island. At 11:44 A.M., Justin was struck by lightning and killed."

In 2012, OSHA fined the park $7,000 indicating park employees didn't follow the procedures for shutting the attractions down when a thunderstorm was in the area. By failing to act, they placed Justin in the path of his fatal lightning strike. The OSHA citation was considered a "serious" violation. Justin's parent's lawsuit is still pending.

The last three stories from Busch Gardens, Tampa have one thing in common; a pre-existing heart condition. In June of 1994, thirteen-year-old Lacy was at the park with her family for a company outing. She pleaded with her mom to stay at the park for one last ride on Kumba— a nearly 3-minute long, steel coaster with inversions and speeds approaching 60 miles per hour.

Kermit Gonzalo

As she waited in line with her friend, Lacy was having second thoughts about riding it, but she went through with it anyway, as she did with several other rides that evening. Sadly, Lacy's ride car pulled back into the loading area, and she was slumped over unconscious in her seat. Paramedics and employees attended to her as fast as possible (as a lawsuit will claim, allegedly not fast enough) and she was rushed to the hospital where she passed away.

The autopsy revealed that Lacey died of neurological cardiac disease, which is an irregular heartbeat brought on by a neurological disorder—she had suffered from seizures in the past and had previously worn a heart monitor. Lacey's family sued the park over the incident. The case went to trial in 1996, and a jury initially awarded the family $500,000 in damages. The jury determined that park workers trained in CPR either didn't or weren't able to get to Lacy fast enough to prevent her from dying.

However, the family was not granted the full amount because the jury found Lacey's mom, Robyn, 30 percent responsible for the death. The jury determined that, based on her prior abuse of drugs, possibly during her pregnancy with Lacey, this may have been a contributing factor to the young girl's health problems.

Roughly six years after Lacey's incident, thirty-year-old Dave did what so many of us do without hesitation each year. He took a ride on a roller coaster. Dave took his ride with a serious health condition unbeknownst to him.

The condition was inherited and caused the coronary arteries of his heart to narrow. Sadly, this condition was revealed when his autopsy was performed. In May of 2000, Dave went to Busch Gardens with a group of friends and co-workers. His day at the park took him to Montu, a soaring inverted steel coaster.

Amusement Park 9-1-1

After leaving the ride, Dave didn't complain of chest pains, but of pains in his stomach. He mentioned he needed to sit down and relax, and separated from his friends. An hour later, Dave's heart stopped pumping normally and he passed away almost instantly. His autopsy revealed his pre-existing condition, along with a previous heart attack, that he was probably unaware he'd had. The medical report stated Dave was a ticking time bomb. While the ride may have affected his heart condition, the incident could have also happened when he was at home lying in bed.

In July of 2006, fifty-two-year-old Thomas was visiting Busch Gardens with his church group. Just before 10 A.M., he boarded the wooden coaster Gwazi—a dueling "old-school" type of coaster. The ride doesn't feature inversions or hyper speeds but can still bring thrills and chills. When Thomas exited the coaster he asked park staff for help. He told them he wasn't feeling well, so First Aid was called. Medical workers arrived and Thomas was initially responsive. He was transported to the hospital, where he passed away two hours later. Physicians determined his cause of death was from a heart attack, as he had hardening of the arteries in his heart and suffered from high blood pressure.

This chapter closes out the situations that played out at some of the more popular nationally recognized amusement parks in the country. The next and final chapter features stories from regional parks. Some are still in existence, some are long gone but all have a tragic story to share.

REGIONAL FAVORITES

All right, so by now, you clearly get it. Accidents happen, as do incidents, acts of God or Mother Nature, sexual assaults, animal attacks, theft, camel punching, and scandals of all sorts. The list could go on and on. Death and disorder looms over the amusement park industry as it does in just about every other facet of life. This book may even have you thinking twice about your next choice of ride when you visit an amusement park.

Freak things don't stop just because we go on vacation or are looking for a day of carefree fun. If anything, maybe our senses are dulled a bit or lulled into a state of submission. Perhaps this relaxation leaves us more vulnerable as we seek refuge in the high speed and thrilling mechanized world of amusement parks.

Whatever dangers or accidents may lurk in America's amusement parks, they are certainly safer than a ride on the "human powered Ferris Wheel" found overseas. When you hear those words, you probably envision a few men standing around cranking away at something mechanical to propel the wheel. Get that image out of your head.

It's actually a handful of men who climb aboard the ride, stand on the outer and inner structure and leap off while holding on to propel it. They use their body weight and gravity to spin the wheel around as riders sit in cars and enjoy the ride. I kid you not, this is quite common in India, Myanmar and other Asian countries where electricity or generators aren't as accessible for a variety reasons. Hey, who are we to judge, right? In countries where people struggle to eat and rise above poverty, ingenuity (not sure if that is the right word here) kicks in to make a buck and to entertain.

A mentioned back in the story about Fabio and the book cover budget, well, the budget for photos was even less! A quick search on Google or YouTube will reveal several examples of the human powered Ferris Wheel.

In keeping with the international theme, you may not know this, but many of the coasters we ride in the States are actually designed and built by European companies. So naturally our international friends are no strangers to amusement park accidents. Across the pond in England one of the most horrific roller coaster accidents ever claimed the lives of five children on May 30, 1972. On the banks of the River Thames in London, sits the 200-acre Battersea Park. The Victorian park dates back to 1854, and today it features lush and exotic gardens along with sporting and recreation fields.

Back in 1951, the park featured the Battersea Fun Fair. The Fun Fair was an amusement park featuring a roaring wooden roller coaster named the Big Dipper. During the years it operated, the coaster was widely considered a fun and safe thrill ride. Aside from an empty car derailment the year the park opened in 1951, there were few, if any, incidents. That changed one afternoon in May of 1972 when a ride car heading towards the top of a 120-foot hill failed to make it up to the apex.

Tragically, the ride cars of the coaster detached from the steel cable that pulled the vehicles to the summit. The cars slowly started to roll backwards; ride operators tried to manually engage the steel break but were unsuccessful. The rogue cars picked up speed and raced towards the right turn in the track. As the coaster sped along wildly, it failed to veer right and derailed, sending the cars crashing into a barrier. Five children were killed and thirteen more were injured. After the accident, the ride was closed down, as was the Fun Fair

Amusement Park 9-1-1

just two short years later in 1974.

The next international story took place closer to home in Edmonton, Alberta, Canada at the West Edmonton Mall. The mall is home to Galaxyland, the world's largest indoor amusement park that features the world's largest indoor triple loop roller coaster, the Mindbender.

The Mindbender debuted in 1985, taking riders on a 70-second trip featuring multiple loops, twists, drops and bends at speeds nearing 60 miles an hour. A year after the ride opened, the coaster was the scene of a terrible accident. On June 14, 1986, a group of mall visitors headed over to what was then known as the Fantasyland Amusement Park (the park was sued by Disney for using their trademark of Fantasyland and it later became Galaxyland) to ride the coaster, Mindbender.

That evening, twelve people took their places in their respective ride cars and set out on their ride. The coaster started out on its course just as it had countless times that year. As the ride went through its big drop, the four cars started to pick up speed. As the speed increased, the last ride car started to fishtail. The bolts from the left inside wheel assembly were missing and the fishtailing car was now off the track as it approached the third and final loop.

Each of the riders held on to their lap bars for dear life. Rod—who was riding in the last car with his friend David—felt the lock on his lap bar release, and he went airborne out of his car as the coaster tried to enter the loop. With the ride car disengaged from the track, it didn't have enough speed to complete the revolution. The car stalled at the top and slid backwards, slamming into a concrete pillar, killing twenty-four-year-old Tony, and his fiancé, twenty-one-year old Cindy, and twenty-four-year-old David. Rod, who was ejected from the ride, survived with two broken legs, a broken pelvis, broken shoulder and a punctured lung. He was hospitalized for six months and had to relearn how to walk.

After the accident, the coaster was closed for several months for an investigation and redesign of the ride cars. The redesigned coaster now features three ride cars instead of four. Seat belts and headrests were added, as well as anti-roll back mechanisms for each ride car. The Mindbender hasn't had an accident since that tragic day in 1986.

The next story brings us back State-side to New Jersey. Any discussion about amusement park accidents wouldn't be complete without mentioning the notorious Action Park in Vernon, New Jersey.

Action Park is located in northern New Jersey roughly 100 miles north of Six Flags Great Adventure. I use the word "is" because the legendary park *is* back in business after being closed for nearly twenty years. Perhaps you're not familiar with Action Park and its dubious legacy. Most people probably aren't unless they grew up in and around northern New Jersey, or within driving distance of the New York metropolitan area during the 1970s through the 1990s.

As NJ.com reminisced, locals lovingly dubbed the park, "Class-Action Park," "Accident Park," and "Traction Park." You can obviously deduce that these names came about because of the amount of accidents at the park. Word even got out in the mid 1980s that the local hospital was seeing 5-10 patients a day from the park. This increase in hospital visits taxed the local ambulance companies so much that the owners of the park had to contribute financially to the town of Vernon for additional ambulances.

The stories about this park are legendary; some tales have been embellished over the years and many have not. With that being said, let's just touch on a few of the low-lights from the water park. Action Park did have non-water based attractions, but most of the unfortunate souls that lost their lives had it happen around water. So let's hop in the time machine and visit 1982.

Amusement Park 9-1-1

That year was a pretty tragic year for the park. The week of July 24, 1982 was a terrible week for Action Park visitors. During this week, the park saw two fatalities. On the 24th, a fifteen-year-old boy drowned in the 100-foot wide by 250-feet long wave pool. The freshwater pool had waves as high as three feet and a capacity of 1,000 swimmers at a time. Sadly, the wave pool earned the nickname "grave pool" as the pool claimed the lives of two more swimmers; in August of 1984, a twenty-year-old man, and in July of 1984, an eighteen-year-old man.

The other fatality during the summer of 1982 was on the Kayak Experience. As the name declares, park-goers hop in a kayak and venture down simulated rapids. At this attraction, submerged electric fans forcefully kept the water moving and created rapids. That summer afternoon, twenty-seven-year-old Jeffrey ventured down the rapids on his trip to the park. Tragically, Jeffrey hopped out of his kayak to correct its course and was electrocuted. While Jeffrey was out of his vessel he came into contact with something electrical and was fatally shocked. Two other people in Jeffrey's vicinity were also shocked but luckily survived the jolt. After Jeffrey's death, the park closed the attraction permanently.

The park was the scene of more deaths and hundreds of more injuries, broken bones and bruises. After all, this was the place that featured "Grass Skiing;" it's exactly what you think it is. Strap on wheeled skis and head down a grassy hill. If that didn't thrill you, you could try your hand at cliff diving or maybe the Alpine Slide, where you sat in a plastic sled and went careening down a concrete track—lots of skin was lost on that adventure.

Last on the head-scratching list would be the aptly named Cannonball Loop. This bad boy was an enclosed water slide, which isn't that unusual. What was unusual was the feature at the end of the slide. The last segment of the Cannonball was the vertical loop, something you would normally see on a roller coaster but not usually on a water slide.

Riders would go down the slide, hopefully pick up enough speed (and have some good water pressure behind them), and travel 360 degrees around the loop and splash into a waiting body of water. During tests of the slide before it opened, test dummies were sent down the ride. Most dummies emerged from the side without their limbs. If that wasn't bad enough, the slide was created with an emergency hatch door to retrieve the folks that didn't make it all the way around. The hatch door wasn't put to use that often, as there were too many complaints of bloody noses, injured backs and an overall reluctance by park visitors to ride it. This led the park to close it down permanently after complaints and inquiries by the State.

As mentioned, 2014 saw the return of the legendary park—or at least something sharing the same name. Welcome back Action Park! Here's to more memories, hopefully less painful ones!

Traveling west from New Jersey, a few states over is Kings Island Amusement Park in Mason, Ohio. Oh boy, where to start with this park. We can start with a few facts and background. The park is located just northwest of Cincinnati, Ohio. It opened in 1972 and today features nearly fifty rides and fourteen roller coasters. It is the 16th most visited park in the country with 3.2 million annual visits.

How about a couple of interesting tidbits? In October of 1975, world famous daredevil, Evel Knievel, jumped fourteen Greyhound buses on his motorcycle. In 2008, Carmen Electra was inducted into the Kings Island hall of fame. Carmen got her start in the entertainment biz as a dancer in the park's show "It's Magic."

Evel and Carmen aside, what may loom largest over this park are the death and accidents over the years—even one of those reality TV ghost shows went to the park to investigate some hauntings back in 2012. Like many other amusement parks today, Kings Island dabbles not only in thrill rides but also water and animal attractions. As we've seen throughout the book, both can be troublesome. In Kings Island's case, their Lion Country Safari had two notable animal incidents.

During the 1970s and into the 1980s, in the region of the park that is now known as Action Zone, a wildlife safari took visitors on an adventure featuring some very large wildlife. One animal group featured on the safari were lions. The big cats didn't maul a park visitor like at Discovery Kingdom. They did, however, have a few run-ins with their trainers and handlers. In July of 1976, a twenty-year-old safari employee was mauled to death by a lion while he was working nearby. Six years later in May of 1982, another worker was attacked by one of the cats, and luckily survived with only scrapes and minor puncture wounds.

One year to the month after the lion attack of 1982, seventeen-year-old John was killed at the park's Grad Night party. The party was held for local students graduating from high school. John was a local track star and had plans on attending Kent State. That evening John was standing in an unauthorized area of an observation platform at the park's replica Eiffel Tower, when he was struck by the elevator's counterweight and fell thirty feet to his death. Eight years would pass until the park was the setting for another serious accident, but when it happened, it happened in a big way.

Ever hear the saying 'bad things happen in threes?' This may have been the case at Kings Island on June 9, 1991. That evening, twenty-two-year-old Timothy and twenty-year-old William both happened to be spending some time over at the Oktoberfest portion of the park. The area debuted in 1972 and resembles a German town. The area is complete with German-inspired architecture, entertainment, food and of course a beer garden near the Oktoberfest Lake. June 9th was just like any other summer evening at the park. That changed around 9:00 P.M. when screaming and splashing were heard. Timothy was in the lake, screaming for help. William and twenty-year-old park security guard Darrel sprang into action and rushed to the lake to rescue Timothy.

At the time, the two men were unaware that Timothy was screaming because he was being electrocuted. Within a matter of moments, the helpful men were also being electrically shocked. All three men were rescued but only one of them made it out alive— it was Timothy. Darrel and William, in performing their good deed, were fatally electrocuted.

A few days later, an investigation revealed the two deaths could have been prevented had a $10 safety device been installed. The local OSHA investigator determined the pond's aerator pump hadn't been grounded properly. In addition, it had a broken ground prong and an oversized circuit breaker that was out of code. More importantly, the pump lacked a ground fault circuit, which would have instantly cut off power when the electrical problem surfaced. Thus $10 would have saved three men from being shocked and two from dying.

At the end of the investigation, OSHA fined the park accordingly: $5,000 for the broken ground plug, $5,000 for the wrong size circuit breaker and failure to protect electrical outlasts near the lake, $5,000 for lack of a ground-fault circuit interrupter, $3,500 for low guard railings on the bridge and deck around the beer garden, $2,500 for inadequate inspections of electrical equipment and $2,500 for damaged waterproof covers on receptacles.

Less than an hour after the accident at the lake, thirty-two-year-old Candy was celebrating her graduation from truck-driving school with some friends. Candy climbed aboard the Flight Commander, a ride that simulated an airplane flight. The pilot or rider used controls to make the two-person car spin or move in many directions, as the ride itself lifts off the ground. Candy was riding alone that night. She was secured into the ride with a shoulder harness and lap bar. At about 60 feet in the air Candy slipped from her restraints, slid to the

Amusement Park 9-1-1

ride's other unoccupied seat and then landed on the ground 30 feet away from the ride. The young mother of two died from her injuries.

Upon investigating the cause of the accident, it was determined that both Candy and a safety defect were the cause of death. It appears Candy was drunk, and her blood alcohol level was three times higher than the legal limit—investigators believe she was unconscious before she fell.

As for the safety defect, the ride had a design flaw. It was possible for a solo rider to slide into the adjacent unoccupied seat, as Candy did. Adjustments came in the way of a higher seat divider and different seat belt in an effort to restrain the person appropriately and safely. Candy's family sued the park and settled out of court confidentially.

The last story from Kings Island doesn't involve an accident on a thrill ride, but is certainly terrifying. In July of 2013, a man was arrested inside the park after visitors reported the suspicious actions of thirty-seven-year-old Robert. Prosecutors believe that Robert may have gone to the park to abduct a child. The police report revealed he walked up to a family and tried to hold their baby as it was acting "fussy." Robert claimed he was trying to help calm the baby down. Mind you, Robert didn't know this family and his actions rightfully scared the family. They contacted park security, who called police to the scene.

When police arrived, they noticed Robert was wearing sunglasses with a video camera attached to them. Apparently, he was using it to record children at the park. Upon searching his semi-tractor trailer—he was a truck driver from Texas—they found children's toys, a police-style baton, a taser, prescription medicine not prescribed to him, a shotgun, two handguns and 4,000 rounds of ammunition.

Wow, 4,000 rounds could have easily gone from child

abduction to mass public shooting or hostage standoff. In November of 2013, Robert copped a no contest plea for having weapons under a disability and a previous felony conviction and drug possession. He was sentenced to 36 months in prison. Crazy stuff there; thankfully the only thing that transpired was some rattled nerves.

Another human-interest story (is your sarcasm detector still on?) comes from Sesame Place back in 2003. An article from the *Philadelphia Inquirer* discussed Sesame Place's dramatic decrease in crime since an increased police presence happened in 2000.

Who knew an amusement park geared towards toddlers and preteens would need big brother, as opposed to big bird, to watch over the park? Sesame Place is a children's amusement park located just outside of Philadelphia and is based on the legendary children's show *Sesame Street*. The folks that bring you SeaWorld currently own the park.

Apparently, back in the year 2000, the park sought help from local police over fifty times during their operating season from May to October. Security at the park was already dealing with an increase in theft from their retail shops, but things got out of hand when petty theft evolved into more serious situations. The park started to see an increase in verbal harassment, pickpocketing, drug possession and violence. Some of the violence featured a fistfight between two mothers at the water park's lazy river. Next, a man repeatedly poked a costumed character with an umbrella in the stomach because he annoyed him. Lastly, there was the incident where a father punched and kicked the Cookie Monster character when he wouldn't pose for a picture with his daughter. Those soccer moms and dads really are a tough crowd!

Finally, the last two stories in Amusement Park 9-1-1 are probably some of the more grossly negligent stories you will read about in the history of amusement parks. One story led to the park's manager being charged with murder over a rider's death. The other resulted in almost instant bankruptcy and closure of a park.

In July of 2003, Ken was taking a trip on the thrill ride, The Hawk at the Rockin Raceway amusement park in Pigeon Forge, Tennessee. The Hawk takes twenty-four riders at a time on a swinging trip from left to right. Then they swing from right to left, climbing higher and higher with each trip (sort of like a pendulum on a clock), reaching heights of over sixty feet. Eventually the swinging back and forth has riders inverted completely upside down. Riders are secured in the ride with a shoulder harness to keep them from falling out.

On Ken's trip, his harness failed and opened up while he was upside down. Thankfully, he was able to brace himself from falling out by pushing his feet against the seat in front of him. After his frightful trip, he notified the park's management who ensured him the ride would be checked and no further trips on it would happen until after an investigation. Ken's story was disregarded and nothing was done about the incident.

Less than a year later in March of 2004, a similar situation happened to June, who was riding the Hawk with her fifteen-year-old son. As June sat down in her seat she decided she wanted to get off. She asked the ride operator to let her out and was told it was too late; the ride was about to start. She called out and said her safety harness wasn't working properly; she received no response from the ride operators and the Hawk started out. Unlike Ken, June was unable to brace herself and hold on for her life. When the ride was at about sixty feet in the air, her harness failed, opened up and she fell to her death.

In the days after the accident, an investigation revealed someone from the park attached two jumper cables to exposed wires in the ride's electrical panel. An engineer determined these cables were installed to bypass the safety system. Basically, someone purposefully rewired the control panel to bypass the safety features of the ride.

When the engineer examined the rigged wiring, he determined that if he removed the black jumper cable, the ride wouldn't operate unless each and every safety restraint was engaged on the ride's seats. When the black jumper cable was reattached, the ride would run regardless if all the safety restraints were engaged.

As the inspecting engineer stated in his report to the state and eventually to the court, "...the accident was a direct result of intentional destruction of the ride safety system."

As the facts of the case unfolded, and as a surprise to many, the state moved to arrest the park's manager and charge him with second degree murder and reckless homicide in June's death—if you remember back to Six Flags Great Adventure in New Jersey, they too were charged in the deaths of eight people after the fire in the Haunted Castle.

The state claimed the park's manager, Charles, pulled the shenanigans of bypassing the safety system to save money on having the ride fixed and maintained properly. The state claimed he was the only one at the park with the knowledge to perform this task. Charles had a background working on missiles during his stint in the Air Force and his previous employment working on nuclear reactors for the Tennessee Valley Authority.

Charles denied these allegations when he took the stand during his own defense in court. He claimed the cables were on the ride from the moment it was delivered in 1998. The ride's manufacturer refuted this statement. The company claimed their field rep visited the park several times between 1998 and 2002 to perform warranty work, and there were no cables attached to the ride during this time. The company went on further and said that after the ride's warranty expired, they didn't hear from Rockin Raceway for additional maintenance work to the Hawk.

In May 2005, the trial wrapped up, and after only a few hours of deliberating, the jury found Charles guilty of reckless homicide, the lesser of the two charges. In July of that year, Charles was sentenced to four years probation with no jail time, 200 hours of community service, and a $5,000 fine.

In December of 2005, June's family settled their $96 million lawsuit against both the park and the ride's maker, Zamperla, with an out of court undisclosed settlement. In the wake of June's accident, the Tennessee Legislature passed a bill requiring owners of amusement rides to have a $1 million insurance policy, and have their rides inspected each year.

Due north from Tennessee is the Hoosier state, Indiana. The state was once home to an amusement park named Old Indiana Fun Park in a town called Thorton. The park opened under a different name in 1985 and struggled to find both its identity and profits over the years. Old Indiana didn't feature record-breaking roller coasters, an enormous wave pool or African safari. What Old Indiana did have was a miniature train. Sounds pretty benign, right? Nope, actually it was just as deadly as any other attraction, or at least any attraction that was lacking appropriate safety mechanisms, braking components or state inspection.

On August 11, 1996, fifty-seven-year-old Nancy took her four-year-old granddaughter (and a half dozen other family members) for a ride on the rails—the miniature rails. As the train started to round a bend, it derailed (an investigation later said the locomotive was traveling faster than the twelve miles per hour it was supposed to) and two of the train cars flipped over.

Nancy was killed when she was thrown from her seat and hit a tree. Her husband suffered a broken leg, her sister a broken arm, and four-year-old granddaughter Emily had a broken neck, jaw, and arm, and she was paralyzed from the chest down.

An inspection of the ride determined there were several mechanical issues with the brakes and anti-derailment devices. Despite these issues, the ride passed two state inspections. State inspections aside, the park was allegedly aware of issues with the train, as it was rumored to have over 75 derailments in the months leading up to the accident.

So why didn't the two safety inspections over three months catch any of the issues with the train? Well, the state safety inspector admitted that he was not qualified to inspect that ride or if he even inspected it at all. This little tidbit ended up costing not only Nancy her life, but Emily a life with paralysis. It also cost the state a lot of money in a settlement with Emily's family.

At the time of Emily's accident, the Indiana legislature felt public pressure to do right by Emily. In 1997 (also the year the park accepted responsibility but denied knowing about the defects of the train and went bankrupt), Governor Frank O'Bannon, lifted the state's tort threshold from $500,000 to $1.5 million for Emily's case.

The state agreed to pay the majority of her medical bills and provide her with ongoing coverage under other state programs. Years later, Emily holds her head high. Her father started the Emily Hunt Foundation, which holds fundraisers such as Emily's Walk to raise money for spinal cord research.

In 1998, she even got the attention of the late Superman himself, Christopher Reeve, with whom the family grew close. Despite all of this adversity, Emily headed off to college in 2011, not allowing any obstacles to get in her way.

This last story was an effort to end an otherwise tragic subject matter with something very inspiring. So what to say about the stories of Amusement Park 9-1-1? If nothing else, it seems as though the book has evolved into a warning guide or reinforcement of being cognizant of any pre-existing health conditions and being aware of entrusting your life to a park's safety record.

Don't be dismissive of the repeated warnings stationed at every amusement park. The warnings are real, as are the potential deadly after-effects for those with a health condition. If there is an inkling that you don't feel right physically, be it the heat of the day, or anything else, opt off the ride; it's not worth it.

If you have another feeling that you aren't safely harnessed into your seat or something isn't right with the ride, be vocal—it's your life—speak up. Better safe than sorry. Lastly, always follow the instructions, rules and use common sense. If you lose your hat (there were actually more of these stories that weren't included), glasses or mobile phone when you're on the ride, leave it. Get a new one on the way home.

This book is in no way complete in regards to the issues at amusement parks. I purposely didn't include, or not include, a park (except for Disney, as explained in the introduction). You name it, big or small, Cedar Point, Knott's Berry Farms, Hershey Park, Dollywood; accidents and incidents are pressing issues the industry deals with routinely.

Whether the industry or the parks acknowledge it publicly or the story makes it into the news, there is a good chance a park-goer experienced some sort of health issue this month or even this week.

These tales of sorrow, pain and regret came from what started out as a day of joy and excitement and ended up in a hospital or with the loss of a loved one. Remember, as the amusement park industry claims and this book has repeated numerous times, the odds may be 1 in 750 million for a fatal accident, but

Kermit Gonzalo

if you are that one, it is 100%.

Happy riding, stay safe and no slapping camels!

SELECTED BIBLIOGRAPHY BY CHAPTER:

CHAPTER ONE:

Bloom, Tracy. "Coroner IDs Man Killed in Universal CityWalk Officer-Involved Shooting." *KTLA 5*. 20 June 2014. Web. 29 June 2014.

FIXED-SITE AMUSEMENT RIDE INJURY SURVEY, 2010 UPDATE. Rep. no. International Association of Amusement Parks and Attractions Alexandria, Virginia. National Safety Council. Print.

Garcia, Jason. "Universal Orlando Tax Breaks: Universal Orlando Claims Millions in Tax Breaks through Program to Help Struggling Neighborhoods." *Orlando Sentinel*. 2 Feb. 203. Web. 29 June 2014.

Jacobson, Susan. "Orlando Man Charged In Rape At Universal Studios." *Orlando Sentinel*. 9 Apr. 2012. Web. 29 June 2014.

Jacobson, Susan. "Universal CityWalk Rape: Man Raped Man He Met in Bar at Universal CityWalk, Orlando Police Say." *Orlando Sentinel*. 9 Apr. 2012. Web. 29 June 2014.

"Landmark Ruling in Handicap Access to Coaster - Will This Affect Future Ride Design? - Entertainment Designer." *Entertainment Designer RSS*. Web. 29 June 2014.

"Leslie Vaughn Killer (1968 - 2003) - Find A Grave Memorial." *Leslie Vaughn Killer (1968 - 2003) - Find A Grave*

Memorial. Web. 29 June 2014.

"Man Dies after Falling at Universal Orlando Ride." *State: Covered Windows Made House an 'oven' in Fatal Fire.* Associated Press, 24 Sept. 2004. Web. 29 June 2014.

Martin, Hugo. "Amputees Kept off Roller Coaster Sue Universal Studios Hollywood." *Los Angeles Times.* Los Angeles Times, 10 July 2012. Web. 29 June 2014.

Mussenden, Sean. "Death On `Mummy' Ride Ruled Accidental." *Orlando Sentinel.* 24 Sept. 2004. Web. 29 June 2014.

Mussenden, Sean. "Fun Day At Park Turns Tragic." *Orlando Sentinel.* 23 Sept. 2004. Web. 29 June 2014.

Ofgang, Kenneth. "Death Penalty Upheld for Man Who Killed Mother on Mother's Day." *Death Penalty Upheld for Man Who Killed Mother on Mother's Day.* 26 Aug. 2008. Web. 29 June 2014. http://www.metnews.com/articles/2008/cara082608.ht.

Palm, Anika. "Tased Man Dies after Scuffle with OPD at Universal Studios Theater." *Orlando Sentinel.* 22 Apr. 2011. Web. 29 June 2014.

Palm, Anika. "Taser Dead Orlando Universal Adam Johnson: Death of Man Tased by OPD Puzzles Family, Fiancée." *Orlando Sentinel.* 22 May 2011. Web. 29 June 2014.

Phillips, Chuck. "MCA Settles Sexual Harassment Lawsuit : Courts: A Former Universal Studios Hollywood Tour Employee Will Receive about $600,000." *Los Angeles Times.* Los Angeles Times, 02 Sept. 1993. Web. 29 June 2014.

Powers, Scott. "Sex Attack Reported at Universal Studios." *Sun Sentinel.* 06 Jan. 2007. Web. 29 June 2014.

Rippel, Amy. "Universal Orlando Closes Coaster As Precaution." *Orlando Sentinel.* Web. 29 June 2014.

Rippel, Amy. "Woman Collapses After `Hulk' Ride." *Sun Sentinel.* 24 Sept. 2003. Web. 29 June 2014.

Rousos, Rick. "Autopsy Concludes Police Restraints Killed Winter Haven Man." *The Ledger*. 16 Mar. 2012. Web.

Serna, Joseph. "Gunfire at Universals CityWalk Sent Visitors Running For Cover." *Los Angeles Times*. Los Angeles Times, 21 May 2014. Web. 29 June 2014.

CHAPTER TWO:

Barker, Tim. "Killer Whale Off Hook." *Orlando Sentinel*. 2 Oct. 1999. Web. 29 June 2014.

Barker, Tim. "Seaworld Settles Sex Litigation." *Orlando Sentinel*. 18 Mar. 2000. Web. 29 June 2014.

Boas, Sherry. "Is Florida Really the Lightning Capital of the World?" *Orlando Sentinel*. 11 June 2006. Web. 29 June 2014.

Chumley, Cheryl K. "PETA Demands Inquiry as SeaWorld Dolphin Bites Girl, 9." *Washington Times*. The Washington Times, 28 Feb. 2014. Web. 29 June 2014.

Clarke, Sara. "SeaWorld Worker Arrested." *Orlando Sentinel*. 21 July 2008. Web. 29 June 2014.

Couwels, John. "SeaWorld Defends Protocol, Staffers' Actions after Dolphin Bites Girl." *CNN*. Cable News Network, 03 Dec. 2012. Web. 29 June 2014.

Curtis, Henry P. "Tourist Dies after He Was Pulled from Water Ride at SeaWorld's Aquatica." *Orlando Sentinel*. 4 Oct. 2010. Web. 29 June 2014.

Edwards, Amy. "SeaWorld Worker Admits to Sex with Boy, Feds Say." *Orlando Sentinel*. 13 Aug. 2010. Web. 29 June 2014.

Edwards, Amy. "SeaWorld Worker Admits to Sex with Boy, Feds Say." *Orlando Sentinel*. 13 Aug. 2010. Web. 29 June 2014.

"Father Dies after Stubbing Toe in Tropical Pool." *The Telegraph*. Telegraph Media Group, 27 Jan. 2009. Web. 29 June 2014.

"Federal Jury Convicts Man of Producing Child Pornography at Sea World." *USDOJ: US Attorney's Office*. Web. 29 June 2014.

Fielding, James. "SeaWorld Whale That 'killed' Three Still Being Used to Breed, Former Worker Claims." *Daily Express World RSS*. 17 Nov. 2013. Web. 29 June 2014.

Flynn, Barry. "Parents Sue Over Death In Park Tank." *Orlando Sentinel*. 21 Sept. 1999. Web. 29 June 2014.

Garcia, Jason. "SeaWorld Sizes up Terror Risk over Chemicals Stored at Park." *Orlando Sentinel*. 11 Dec. 2008. Web. 29 June 2014.

Garcia, Jason. "SeaWorld Sizes up Terror Risk over Chemicals Stored at Park." *Orlando Sentinel*. 11 Dec. 2008. Web. 29 June 2014.

Gorman, Ryan. "SeaWorld Dolphin Bites Nine-year-old Girl during Family Visit to Texas Park." *Mail Online*. Associated Newspapers, 28 Feb. 2014. Web. 29 June 2014.

Graaf, Mia De. "Revealed: SeaWorld Whales Are Pumped with Valium and Xanax to Control Their Aggressive Behavior as Animal Rights Group Say 'it's the Final Straw' for Crisis-hit Park." *Mail Online*. Associated Newspapers, 03 Apr. 2014. Web. 29 June 2014.

Harris, Sheryl. "Mechanical Failure Blamed for Sea World Boat Accident That Injured 23.(Originated from Knight-Ridder Newspapers)." *- Knight Ridder/Tribune News Service*. 18 Aug. 1996. Web. 29 June 2014.

"Holidaymaker Died after Stubbing His Toe on Coral." *Metro Holidaymaker Died after Stubbing His Toe Oncoral Comments*. Web. 29 June 2014.

"Incidents between Humans and Killer Whales in Captivity -a Longer List than the Parks Would like to Tell You!" *Incidents between Humans and Killer Whales in Captivity*. Web. 27 June 2014. <http://www.orcahome.de/incidents.htm>.

Kropko, M. R. "Patrons Injured in Sea World Show Boat Accident." *Associated Press.* 17 Aug. 1996. Web.

Levenson, Bob. "Parents Blame Sea World For Son's Death." *Orlando Sentinel.* 1 Apr. 1992. Web. 29 June 2014.

Levenson, Bob. "Sea World Gets Half The Blame." *Orlando Sentinel.* 4 Apr. 1992. Web. 29 June 2014.

"Man Dies after Toe Stub on Coral." *BBC News.* BBC, 29 Jan. 2009. Web. 29 June 2014.

Maxwell, Scott. "Scott Maxwell: SeaWorld Dolphin Bites Girl — No Surprise." *Orlando Sentinel.* 4 Dec. 2012. Web. 29 June 2014.

"Mechanical Failure Blamed for Boat Accident at Sea World." *Associated Press.* 18 Aug. 1996. Web.

Meyers, Anika. "Tourist Who Died after Being Pulled from Aquatica Ride May Have Died of Natural Causes." *Orlando Sentinel.* 5 Oct. 2010. Web. 29 June 2014.

Narain, Jaya. "'Unlucky' Father-of-two Died after Stubbing His Toe on Coral at Florida Theme Park." *Mail Online.* Associated Newspapers, 29 Jan. 2009. Web. 29 June 2014.

"OSHA Fines SeaWorld for Worker Safety Issues following Orca Trainer's Death." *The Los Angeles Times.* 23 Aug. 2010. Web.

"Park Is Sued Over Death of Man in Whale Tank." *The New York Times.* The New York Times, 20 Sept. 1999. Web. 29 June 2014.

Pavuck, Amy. "Child Pornography Sentence: Brandon Schill Sentenced to Federal Prison in Child-porn Case." *Orlando Sentinel.* 16 May 2011. Web. 29 June 2014.

Powers, Scott. "Theme-park Lawsuits: Questions of Safety Go Unsettled." *Orlando Sentinel.* 29 Mar. 2009. Web. 29 June 2014.

Reporter, Daily Mail. "British Holidaymaker Dies after Being Found Face down in Water Rapids Ride at Florida SeaWorld." *Mail Online.* Associated Newspapers. Web. 29 June 2014.

Reuters. "SeaWorld Loses Appeal in Trainer Safety Case."

Metro Papers. 11 Apr. 2014. Web.

Salem, Dina Abou. "SeaWorld Dolphin Bites Girl, Prompts PETA Probe Request." *ABC News*. ABC News Network, 27 Feb. 2014. Web. 29 June 2014.

Savino, Lenny. "Man In Whale Tank Was Drifter." *Orlando Sentinel*. 8 July 1999. Web. 29 June 2014.

Spitz, Jorden. "Safety Is Reviewed At 4 Sea World Parks After Ohio Accident." *Orlando Sentinel*. 20 Aug. 1996. Web. 29 June 2014.

"Trouble at Sea(World): Problems Mount as Dolphin Bites Girl." *PETA Trouble at SeaWorld Problems Mount as Dolphin Bites Girl Comments*. 26 Feb. 2014. Web. 29 June 2014.

Walden, Tiffany. "SeaWorld Orlando Worker Arrested for Stealing Money from Parked Baby Strollers." *Orlando Sentinel*. 14 May 2014. Web. 29 June 2014.

Weiner, Jeff. "SeaWorld Discovery Cove Lightning: Injuries Reported after Lightning Strike at Seaward Discovery Cove." *Orlando Sentinel*. 17 Aug. 2011. Web. 29 June 2014.

"Whales Collide, 1 Is Fatally Injured in Sea World Tank." *Los Angeles Times*. Los Angeles Times, 22 Aug. 1989. Web. 29 June 2014.

CHAPTER THREE:

"2013 Themed Entertainment Association." *2013 Global Attractions Attendance Report*. Web.

Ailworth, Erin. "Six Flags Agrees to Settle Discrimination Suit." *Los Angeles Times*. Los Angeles Times, 14 May 2004. Web. 29 June 2014.

"Amusement Park Victim Identified." *7NEWS*. 28 May 2002. Web. 29 June 2014.

AP. "An 11-year-old Boy Collapsed While..." *Orlando Sentinel*. 21 July 1989. Web. 29 June 2014.

AP. "3 KILLED, 1 INJURED WHEN SIX FLAGS GONDOLA

FALLS." Alton Telegraph, Illinois, 7 July 1978. Web. 29 June 2014.
AP. "Coroner Blames Heart Condition for Girl's Death at Six Flags." *Nwitimes.com*. 06 Dec. 2003. Web. 29 June 2014.
AP. "Park Worker Killed by Roller Coaster." *CJOnline.com*. 11 Apr. 2001. Web. 29 June 2014.
AP. "Roller Coaster Death Under Investigation, Six Flags Ride Closed." *The Southeast Missourian*. 9 July 1984. Web. 29 June 2014.
AP. "Three Hurt in Shooting outside Six Flags Over Georgia." - *Wistv.com*. 5 July 2006. Web. 29 June 2014.
AP. "USATODAY.com - Woman Killed at Six Flags New Orleans." *USATODAY.com - Woman Killed at Six Flags New Orleans*. 11 July 2003. Web. 29 June 2014.
AP. "Woman Flung to Death From Roller Coaster." *The New York Times*. The New York Times, 08 July 1984. Web. 29 June 2014.
AP. "Woman Killed at Six Flags New Orleans." *Woman Killed at Six Flags New Orleans*. 11 July 2003. Web. 29 June 2014.
AP. "Woman's Size Might Have Contributed to Accident." *Newspapers.com*. 18 July 1984. Web. 29 June 2014.
Arthur, Myra. "Man Makes Alleged Sexual Contact with Girl at Fiesta Texas." *Ksat.com*. 24 June 2013. Web.
Avery, Ron. "Violence Shuts Great Adventure Early." *Philly.com*. 20 Apr. 1987. Web. 29 June 2014.
Borg, Gary. "Park Worker Killed By Roller Coaster." *Chicago Tribune*. 31 May 1996. Web. 29 June 2014.
"Camel Attack No Great Adventure." *Reading Eagle*. Associated Press, 17 Sept. 1987. Web. 29 June 2014.
Campisi, Gloria. "Accidents, Violence Mar Park's 13-year History." *Philly.com*. 18 June 1987. Web. 29 June 2014.
Christian, Carol. "Report Details Fatal Roller Coaster Fall."

Houston Chronicle. 11 Nov. 2013. Web. 29 June 2014.

Chu, Henry. "Roller Coaster Worker Dies at Magic Mountain." *Los Angeles Times.* Los Angeles Times, 31 May 1996. Web. 29 June 2014.

Chu, Henry. "Roller Coaster Worker Dies at Magic Mountain." *Los Angeles Times.* Los Angeles Times, 31 May 1996. Web. 29 June 2014.

Ciokajlo, Mickey. "Family Settles Six Flags Suit." *Chicago Tribune.* 29 Mar. 2002. Web. 29 June 2014.

Collins, Calvert. "Woman Fell 75 Feet in Texas Giant Death." *Six Flags: Woman Died While Riding Texas Giant.* 23 July 2013. Web. 29 June 2014.

Comerford, Michael S. "Daily Herald | OSHA Cites Six Flags with 38 Safety Violations." *Daily Herald | OSHA Cites Six Flags with 38 Safety Violations.* Daily Herald, 10 Sept. 2007. Web. 29 June 2014. <http://prev.dailyherald.com/story/?id=34947>.

"CPS Teacher Pleads Guilty in Great America Video Case." *Chicago Breaking News.* 28 Sept. 2010. Web. 29 June 2014. <http://articles.chicagobreakingnews.com/2010-09-28/news/28518038_1_amusement-park-great-america-teacher>.

Eiserer, Tanya. "Family Identifies Dallas Resident Who Was Victim of Texas Giant Accident." *The Dallas Morning News.* 19 July 2013. Web. 29 June 2014.

"Excerpts of Kaitlyn Lasitter's Deposition." *The Courier-Journal.* 30 Jan. 2008. Web. 29 June 2014. <http://www.courier-journal.com/article/20080130/NEWS01/80130056/Excerpts-Kaitlyn-Lasitter-s-deposition>.

Freedman, Rich. "Dakar Just Miffed." *Timesheraldonline.com.* 11 May 2008. Web. 29 June 2014.

Fritz, Mark. "Thrill-a-Minute Can Mean Spill-a-Minute." *Los Angeles Times.* Los Angeles Times, 01 Sept. 1996. Web. 29 June 2014.

Garcia, Kenneth. "2 Marine World Trainers Attacked by

Cougars / One Man Badly Clawed, Hospitalized." *SFGate*. 8 Jan. 1996. Web. 29 June 2014.

Gilbert, Susan. "When Brain Trauma Is at the Other End Of the Thrill Ride." *The New York Times*. The New York Times, 24 June 2002. Web. 29 June 2014.

"Girl Dies After Collapsing At Six Flags." *CBS2 Chicago*. 17 Aug. 2006. Web.

"Girl Likely Choked to Death on Rollercoaster." *ABC News*. ABC News Network, 06 May 2014. Web. 29 June 2014.

Goodyear, Charile. "Bad Cable Blamed in Marine World Ride Failure." *SFGate*. 4 Sept. 1999. Web. 29 June 2014.

Goodyear, Charlie. "Marine World Blamed in Girl's Accident / 4-year-old Wasn't Seated Correctly, Sign Not Posted at Ride, Report Concludes." *SFGate*. 24 Aug. 2002. Web. 29 June 2014.

Goodyear, Charlie. "Previous Accident Blamed on Valve / Marine World's 'Starfish' Shut down." *SFGate*. 11 June 2002. Web. 29 June 2014.

"Gored Elephant Trainer in Critical Condition." *Los Angeles Times*. Los Angeles Times, 02 June 2004. Web. 29 June 2014.

Guccione, Jean. "Bias Suits Hit Magic Mountain." *Los Angeles Times*. Los Angeles Times, 06 Aug. 2001. Web. 29 June 2014.

Hanley, Robert. "GREAT ADVENTURE TRYING TO REGAIN LOST CUSTOMERS." *The New York Times*. The New York Times, 29 July 1987. Web. 29 June 2014.

Harkinson, Josh. "Thrilled to Death." *Houston News and Events*. 03 June 2004. Web. 29 June 2014.

"He Dared To Be Happy." *Hartford Courant*. 07 May 2006. Web. 29 June 2014. <http://articles.courant.com/2006-05-07/features/0605050428_1_cerebral-palsy-second-step-thin/4>.

Heinz, Frank. "Esparza's Family Asks for Sanctions Against Six Flags." *NBC 5 Dallas-Fort Worth*. 15 Feb. 2014. Web. 29 June 2014.

Hull, Bryson. "Corpus Christi Online - / One Dead, Others Injured in Amusement Park Accident." *Corpus Christi Online - / One Dead, Others Injured in Amusement Park Accident*. 22 Mar. 1999. Web. 29 June 2014.

"Investigators Preparing Report In Roller Coaster Death." *NBC30 News*. 4 May 2004. Web. <http://www.nbc30.com/news/3260041/detail.html>.

James, Michael S., and Alexis Shaw. "Witnesses on Six Flags Over Texas Roller Coaster Death: 'That Could Have Been Me'" *ABC News*. ABC News Network, 20 July 2013. Web. 29 June 2014.

Janson, Donald. "GREAT ADVENTURE'S SISTER PARK INSTALLED SPRINKLERS." *The New York Times*. The New York Times, 20 June 1985. Web. 29 June 2014.

Janson, Donald. "PATRONS ENTERED HAUNTED HOUSE AS FIRE BURNED." *The New York Times*. The New York Times, 13 June 1985. Web. 29 June 2014.

Kopenec, Stephanie. "Witness: Six Flags Workers Stood By." Associated Press, 24 Mar. 1999. Web.

LaPlante, Matthew. "Dead Utah Elephant Suffered Tragic Life - and She Wasn't Alone." *Salt Lake Tribune*. 16 Sept. 2008. Web. 29 June 2014.

LaPlante, Matthew. "Former Trainer Says Euthanized Elephant 'lost Her Will' to Live." *ContraCostaTimes.com*. 22 Sept. 2008. Web. 29 June 2014.

Lee, Henry. "Marine World Says 9-Year-Old Boy at Fault for Fall From Ride." *SFGate*. 7 June 1999. Web. 29 June 2014.

Liu, Caitlin. "Family Sues Amusement Park Owner Over Death." *Los Angeles Times*. Los Angeles Times, 23 May 2002. Web. 29 June 2014.

MacDonald, Brandy. "Six Flags Magic Mountain to Reclaim Coaster Title." *Los Angeles Times*. Los Angeles Times, 2 May 2012. Web. 29 June 2014.

"Man Dies After Riding Goliath Roller Coaster at Six Flags Over Georgia." *Fox News*. FOX News Network, 28

July 2006. Web. 29 June 2014.

Mellen, Karen. "2 Girls Injured On Great America Ride." *Chicago Tribune*. 20 July 2000. Web. 29 June 2014.

Murphy, Kim. "Court Says Magic Mountain Can't Deny Request for Gays-Only Night." *Los Angeles Times*. Los Angeles Times, 11 July 1986. Web. 29 June 2014.

Nevious, CW. "Tiger Attack Reminds Us How times Have Changed." *SFGate*. 20 Jan. 2007. Web. 29 June 2014.

"NFPA Journal." *The Haunted Castle, Revisited -*. Web. 29 June 2014. <http://www.nfpa.org/newsandpublications/nfpa-journal/2014/may-june-2014/features/the-haunted-castle-revisited>.

Nielson, John. "6 Stabbed in Gang Fight at Magic Mountain Park." *Los Angeles Times*. Los Angeles Times, 21 June 1985. Web. 29 June 2014.

Nye, James. "'There Was Feathers and Blood Everywhere': Boy's Shock after Being Hit in the FACE by Bird on World's Tallest Rollercoaster." *Mail Online*. Associated Newspapers, 29 July 2012. Web. 29 June 2014.

Owens, Marjorie. "Lawyers: Six Flags Attendant Worked Less than a Week before Fatal Accident." *WFAA Wfaa.com*. 14 Jan. 2014. Web. 29 June 2014.

A, P. "Roller Coaster Harness Blamed in Rider's Death." *Los Angeles Times*. Los Angeles Times, 19 June 1987. Web. 29 June 2014.

Pow, Helen. "Mom Was Flung to Her Death from Six Flags Rollercoaster after 'harness Didn't Come All the Way down in Car Operators Knew Was Faulty'" *Mail Online*. Associated Newspapers, 12 Nov. 2013. Web. 29 June 2014.

"The Region; OSHA Cites Park In Coaster Fatality." *The New York Times*. The New York Times, 26 Aug. 1981. Web. 29 June 2014.

Resnik, Virginia. "Woman, 19, Dies In Fall From Roller

Coaster." *Philly.com.* 18 June 1987. Web. 29 June 2014.

Rhahimi, Shadi. "Arrests Followed Slap of Camel." *PressDemocrat.com.* 7 May 2008. Web. 29 June 2014.

Rogers, Patrick. "Riding for a Fall." *PEOPLE.com.* 20 Sept. 1999. Web. 29 June 2014.

Satzman, Darrell. "Gang Member Hasn't Been Charged With Teen's Death." *Los Angeles Times.* Los Angeles Times, 11 June 1998. Web. 29 June 2014.

"SECURITIES AND EXCHANGE COMMISSION." *Six Flags Inc. Form 8-K.* 2003. Web. 29 June 2014.

Shoichet, Catherine E. "Texas Roller Coaster Set to Reopen after Woman's Death." *CNN.* Cable News Network, 01 Jan. 1970. Web. 29 June 2014.

"Shouka Six Flags Killer Whale Attacks Trainer." *Without Me There Is No You.* Web. 29 June 2014.

"Six Flags Haunted Castle Fire Remembered 30 Years Later." *Six Flags Haunted Castle Fire Remembered 30 Years Later.* Web. 29 June 2014.

"Six Flags Peeping Tom Receives Sentencing - CBS St. Louis." *CBS St Louis.* 14 June 2013. Web. 29 June 2014. www.stlouis.cbslocal.com/2013/06/14six-flags-peeping.com

"Six Flags Worker Hit by Ride Dies." *Chicago Tribune.* 18 June 2004. Web. 29 June 2014.

Tedesco, John. "Report Finds Amusement Parks Didn't Report Injuries." *Houston Chronicle.* 27 June 2009. Web. 29 June 2014.

Uhlinger, Dan. "'I Totally Had Him And Then ... '" *Hartford Courant.* 06 May 2004. Web. 29 June 2014. <http://articles.courant.com/2004-05-06/news/0405060190_1_roller-coaster-amusement-park-rides-accident>.

Wharton, David. "Roller Coaster Worker Broke Rule, Officials Say." *Los Angeles Times.* Los Angeles Times, 01 June 1996. Web. 29 June 2014.

Wiley, Nikki. "Family Awarded $35M in Six Flags Beating Case - MARIETTA - Six Flags over Georgia and Four of Its Former Employees Have Been Ordered to Pay $35 Million to the Family of a Man Who Suffered a Traumatic Brain Injury from a Beating He Received by a Si..." *The Marietta Daily Journal.* 22 Nov. 2013. Web. 29 June 2014.

"Worker Killed in Accident at Six Flags Over Georgia." *North Georgia News.* 27 May 2002. Web. 29 June 2014.

Zhou, Kelly. "Shouka, 'World's Loneliest Whale,' Relocated to SeaWorld San Diego to Live With Fellow Orcas." *TakePart.* 23 Aug. 2012. Web. 29 June 2014.

CHAPTER FOUR:

AP. "Busch Gardens Patron Had Health Issues." *Fox News.* FOX News Network, 26 July 2006. Web. 29 June 2014.

"BOURASSA v. BUSCH ENTERTAINMENT CORP." *Findlaw.* 7 Apr. 2006. Web. 29 June 2014.

Collins, Dan. "Lion Tears Off Zookeeper's Arm." *CBSNews.* CBS Interactive, 2 May 2002. Web. 29 June 2014.

Collins, Matt. "Busch Gardens Worker Arrested for Stealing Brass Used for Roller Coaster Brakes." *WFTS, ABC Tampa.* 3 Aug. 2011. Web. 29 June 2014.

Dujardin, Peter. "Gropings Lawsuit: Busch Gardens Faces $5.3M Lawsuit in Groping Case at Water Country USA." *Daily Press.* 01 June 2011. Web. 29 June 2014.

"Flash Facts About Lightning." *National Geographic.* National Geographic Society, 24 June 2005. Web. 27 June 2014.

Gazella, Katherine. "Northpinellas: Death at Theme Park Stuns Friends." *Northpinellas: Death at Theme Park Stuns Friends.* 30 May 2000. Web. 29 June 2014.

Kelly, Ashley. "Federal Trial Scheduled in Busch Gropings

Lawsuit." *Daily Press*. 12 Dec. 2011. Web. 29 June 2014.

Kelly, Ashley. "Jury Rules Busch Not Liable in $5.3 Million Sexual Assault Case." *Daily Press*. 14 Dec. 2011. Web. 29 June 2014.

Liberto, Jennifer. "'Vicious' Peacocks or Ordinary Birds?" *Tampabay Times*. 9 July 2005. Web. 29 June 2014.

Mitchell, Robbyn. "Adventure Island Employee Dies after Being Struck by Lightning." *Tampa Bay Times*. 10 Sept. 2011. Web. 29 June 2014.

Mussenden, Sean. "Finger In Cage Incited Lion To Bite." *Orlando Sentinel*. 14 May 2002. Web. 29 June 2014.

"On Responsibility and Deep Pockets - Tampa Bay Business Journal." *Tampa Bay Business Journal*. 24 June 1996. Web. 29 June 2014.

Reyes, Ray. "Adventure Island Sued in Staffer's Death." *TBO.com*. 3 Aug. 2013. Web. 29 June 2014.

Sullivan, Dan. "Father Recalls Adventure Island Lifeguard, USF Student Struck by Lightning." *Tampa Bay Times*. 11 Sept. 2011. Web. 29 June 2014.

"Suspect Arrested For Selling Brass Plates." *Hillsborough County Sheriff's Office - 11-261*. Hillsborough County Sheriff's Office District 4 Detectives Step up Their Metal Theft Initiative., 3 Aug. 2011. Web. 29 June 2014.

Vansickle, Abbie. "Man Dies after Roller Coaster Ride." *Tampabay.com*. 26 July 2006. Web. 29 June 2014.

Ward, Taylor. "Girl Killed on Tampa Roller Coaster." *Lakeland Ledger*. 12 June 1995. Web. 29 June 2014.

Wee, Eric. "During Photo Shoot Fabio Does More Than Look At Birdie." *Washington Post*. N.p., 31 Mar. 1999. Web. 29 June 2014.

CHAPTER FIVE:

"Action Park To Return At Mountain Creek Resort In New Jersey - CBS New York." *CBS New York.* 3 Apr. 2014. Web. 29 June 2014.

"ALEXANDER v. ZAMPERLA." *Court of Appeals of Tennessee, at Knoxville. May 20, 2010 Session. Filed August 27, 2010.* Web.

AP. "18-Year-Old Drowns At Amusement Park." *The New York Times.* The New York Times, 19 July 1987. Web. 29 June 2014.

AP. "3 ARE KILLED IN ACCIDENTS AT OHIO AMUSEMENT PARK." *DeseretNews.com.* 10 June 1991. Web. 29 June 2014.

AP. "3 Die in Mishaps At Ohio Fun Park Over Weekend." *Pittsburgh Post-Gazette.* 11 June 1991. Web. 29 June 2014.

AP. "3 Hurled to Death in Canada as Roller Coaster Derails in Mall." *Los Angeles Times.* Los Angeles Times, 16 June 1986. Web. 29 June 2014.

AP. "Alcohol Factor Studied In Fatal Plunge At Park." *Toledo-Blade.* 19 June 1991. Web. 29 June 2014.

AP. "Inexpensive Device Could Have Prevented Deaths." *Daily News, Bowling Green Kentucky.* 12 June 1991. Web. 29 June 2014.

AP. "Lions Kill Safari Ranger." *Lions Kill Safari Ranger.* Florence Times Daily, 26 July 1976. Web. 29 June 2014.

AP. "No Mechanical Flaw Found on Death RIde." *Lodi News-Sentinel.* 19 June 1991. Web. 29 June 2014.

AP. "One Elephant Kills Trainer, Second Takes People On Wild Ride." *One Elephant Kills Trainer, Second Takes People On Wild Ride.* 6 Feb. 1989. Web. 29 June 2014.

AP. "Park Closes Ride After Patron Dies." *The New York Times.* The New York Times, 02 Aug. 1982. Web. 29 June

2014.

AP. "Park Deaths Could Have Been Avoided." *Gadsden Times*. 13 June 1991. Web. 29 June 2014.

AP. "Park Injury Settlement Costs State $1.5 Million." *Toledo Blade*. 27 Feb. 1997. Web. 29 June 2014.

AP. "Reeve Offers Hope To Paralyzed Youngster." *Sarasota Herald-Tribune*. 5 Oct. 1998. Web. 29 June 2014.

AP. "Teen Dies From Fall At Amusement Park." *The Bryan Times*. 10 May 1983. Web. 29 June 2014.

AP. "Train Derails At Fun Park, Kills 1, Badly Injures Girl, 4." *Orlando Sentinel*. 12 Aug. 1996. Web. 29 June 2014.

AP. "USATODAY.com - Amusement Park Death Leads to Tennessee Murder Trial." *USATODAY.com - Amusement Park Death Leads to Tennessee Murder Trial*. 10 May 2005. Web. 29 June 2014.

Augenstein, Seth. "A Blast from the Past: 'Action Park' Is Back for the Summer." *NJ.com*. 3 Apr. 2014. Web. 29 June 2014.

"Battersea Park." *- Battersea London SW11 4NJ*. Web. 29 June 2014.

"Brooklyn Man Drowns in Pool At a Jersey Amusement Park." *The New York Times*. The New York Times, 26 Aug. 1984. Web. 29 June 2014.

"Defendant Takes Stand in Ride Death Trial." Wate.com, 14 May 2005. Web. 29 June 2014.

Evans, Tim. "Ind. Lawmaker: $5M Not Enough for Stage Collapse Victims." *USATODAY.COM*. 22 Sept. 2011. Web. 29 June 2014.

"Family Settles in Rockin' Raceway Suit." *Seymour Herald Newspaper*. 23 Dec. 2005. Web. 29 June 2014.

Franklin, Jasmine. "Mindbender Tragedy, 25 Years Later." *Edmonton Sun*. 14 June 2011. Web.

"Galaxyland." *West Edmonton Mall -*. Web. 29 June 2014.

Hirsch, Chelsea. "New Jersey's Action Park to Debut ZERO-G Water Slide with a Nearly 1,000-foot Drop." *NY Daily News*. 21 June 2014. Web. 29 June 2014.

"I Survived Londons Big Dipper." *I Survived London's Big*

Dipper Crash. 23 Mar. 2013. Web. 29 June 2014.

"Indiana Tort Claims Act | Jamesludlowatty.com." *Jamesludlowatty.com.* Web. 29 June 2014.

"KI Hall of Fame." *Largest Amusement & Waterpark in the Midwest.* Web. 29 June 2014. <https://www.visitkingsisland.com/online-fun/ki-hall-of-fame>.

"Knott's Closes Its XK-1 Ride After Park Death in Ohio." *Los Angeles Times.* Los Angeles Times, 12 June 1991. Web. 29 June 2014.

"London's Forgotten Disasters: The Battersea Big Dipper Crash." *Londonist.* 4 Mar. 2014. Web. 29 June 2014. <http://londonist.com/2014/03/londons-forgotten-disasters-the-battersea-big-dipper-crash.php>.

"Manager Charged with Murder in Pigeon Forge Ride Death." *Manager Charged with Murder in Pigeon Forge Ride Death.* 29 Sept. 2004. Web. 29 June 2014.

"Manager Convicted of Reckless Homicide in Ride Death." 16 May 2005. Web. 29 June 2014.

"Old Indiana Fun Park [Thorntown]." *Lost Indiana.* Web. 29 June 2014. <http://lostindiana.net/2001/02/01/old-indiana-fun-park-thorntown/>.

Parnes, Amie. "Crime at Sesame Place Has Fallen since 2000 Heightened Surveillance and an Increased Police Presence Have Helped Make the Park Safer." *Philly.com.* 11 Aug. 2003. Web. 29 June 2014.

"Pigeon Forge Amusement Park Manager Avoids Jail Time." Wate.com, 26 July 2005. Web. 29 June 2014.

"Prosecutor: Man Arrested at Kings Island Had 4,000 Rounds of Ammo in Truck." *WLWT 5.* 11 July 2013. Web.

"Son Testifies in Pigeon Forge Ride Death Trial." *Son Testifies in Pigeon Forge Ride Death Trial.* 12 May 2005. Web. 29 June 2014.

Stehr, John. "Ball State Instructor Inspires Accident Survivor to Pursue Fashion Dream." *Ball State Instructor Inspires Accident Survivor to Pursue Dream.* WTHR.com, 11 May 2011. Web. 29 June 2014.

"Texas Man Going to Prison for Kings Island Crime." *WHIO.*

com. 7 Nov. 2013. Web.

"There Was Nothing in the World Like Action Park." *Sometimes Interesting.* Web. 29 June 2014.

Vickery, Hugh. "DESPITE RECENT DEATHS, PARKS SAY RIDES ARE SAFE." *DeseretNews.com.* Aug. 1991. Web. 29 June 2014.

"Woman Dies in Fall from Pigeon Forge Amusement Ride." *Wate.com.* 14 Mar. 2004. Web. 29 June 2014.

"Woman Killed When Train Derails At Amusement Park." *Sun Journal.* 12 Aug. 1996. Web. 29 June 2014.

ABOUT THE AUTHOR

Kermit Gonzalo was born and raised near the Texas Panhandle. As a boy growing up, he spent his summers traveling the country with his family exploring the nation's amusement parks.

Over the years he has become a self-anointed roller coaster junkie. When he isn't visiting amusement parks, he works in the health care industry. He currently resides in Florida with his wife, two kids, two dogs and two cats.

Made in the USA
Las Vegas, NV
21 March 2023